English Extra

Extra

Teacher's
Manual
by
SUSAN GAER

GRACE TANAKA AND KAY FERRELL

PRENTICE HALL REGENTS

Upper Saddle River, NJ 07458

Publisher: Mary Jane Peluso
Development Editor: Carol Callahan
Electronic production: Noël Vreeland Carter
Interior design: Carey Davies and Noël Vreeland Carter
Manufacturing Manager: Ray Keating
Art Director: Merle Krumper
Interior Art: Carey Davies
Cover Design: Carey Davies

12 13 OPM 09 08 07

ISBN 0-13-870114-8

Contents

Unit

Introduction

Welcome to **English Extra.** This beginning ESL textbook gives adult learners a comprehensive set of communication skills in the English language. Throughout each unit, language is natural, authentic, and contextualized in situations with which your beginning learners of the English language can identify. In **English Extra** oral skills, such as listening and speaking as well as reading and writing, are progressively developed.

Tapescripts of material that does not appear on the student pages are provided in the back of the student book. If you have access to an overhead projector, it's a good idea to make transparencies of each page of the book whenever possible as an aid so you can model/present the lesson and the students can follow along.

UNIT OVERVIEW

Listen and read.

Each opening page begins with a large, colorful illustration and text (conversation balloons, vocabulary words, a short paragraph about the illustration, etc.). All unit openers are designed to encourage students to use their own experiences and language to talk about a specific topic. Below are basic techniques that can be used with the opener page:

Allow students to "talk" to each other about the picture. Encourage students to respond to questions. Restate their ideas in acceptable English and write your words/phrases, or sentences on the board. Then read aloud what you have written.

Next, ask questions about the picture. Begin with some general questions, such as the following:

For most beginning students:

1. Are there 1 or 2 people?
2. Are they in a school or a hospital?
3. Is he/she from the USA or Asia?
4. Are they talking or working?

For low beginning students:

1. How many people are there?
2. Where are they?
3. Where are they from?
4. What are they doing?

Elicit as much information about the picture as possible. Use commands and questions interchangeably, such as *Point to the men. Are there two people or three people in this picture? How many people are there in this picture?* (See each specific unit for detailed questions.)

Before moving on to the text, students should have a complete understanding of 1, what is happening, and 2, most of the language that will appear in the text. (See each specific unit for detailed questions.)

Presentation instructions.

Play the tape and have students listen (or read when asked). Read the text aloud. Use an overhead transparency, if available, to point out each word you say. Have the students read each word after you. Repeat this procedure two or three times with the students.

Practice instructions.

Ask the students to practice the text in pairs or small groups (See each unit for specific details.) As students practice in pairs, walk around the room while they are practicing to listen and review any problems they may have in pronunciation.

Review pages.

These are placed randomly throughout the book to reinforce already learned vocabulary, oral language, and structures. These pages can usually be covered quite quickly using the tapescript. If possible, make a transparency of each page to follow along with the tape. See each unit for more specific information.

Vocabulary pages.

All units have pages that introduce vocabulary.

If possible, make a transparency of each page and follow along with the tape. Point to the picture on the transparency as students point to each word.

Practice.

Ask students to cover the words at the bottom of the page. (Show students how to make and use a paper guide to move down the page.) Using the overhead transparency, ask students to point to the pictures of various words. Then put students into pairs and have them point to various words. (*Example:* Student 1 says, *"Point to the bookcase."* Student 2 points.)

Optional follow-up.

Using a crossword puzzle creator or a wordsearch creator, make a crossword puzzle or wordsearch game. If students have access to computers, encourage each group to make the puzzle to give to another group.

Vocabulary reinforcement/structure.

Grammatical structure is practiced implicitly in context throughout the textbook. It is up to each individual teacher how much additional grammar is introduced to the class. Structure is introduced along with vocabulary.

I can do this!

At the end of every unit is a checklist of objectives that the students should have mastered.

Explain to students the meaning of the title. Then choose whichever method of evaluation that you wish to use. There are a variety of ways this page can be used. Here are a few examples.

1. *For self evaluation:* Have students go over the page and put a check in front of each competency they feel they have learned in this unit.
2. *For peer evaluation:* Have peers test each other. Show students simple ways to ask their partner to use the expressions covered in the unit.
3. *For teacher assessment:* Assess students' understanding of vocabulary words by asking them to label the objects they stand for.

Jazz Chants.

Please see page 17 of the workbook for an example of the Jazz Chant entitled *Ice Cream.* Divide the class into two groups. Assign a part of the Jazz Chant to each of two groups. This can be done by alternating lines or by stanzas. Jazz Chants can also be done as a whole class activity. As a whole class activity the teacher can read part and have the students echo the teacher.

General Beginning Level Techniques

Information-gap activities.

In Information-gap activities, students are either in pairs or small groups. Each pair is given two different pages, one labeled *A* and the other labeled *B*. The object is for students to find out the information on their partner's paper by asking questions. For this activity to be successful at the beginning level, questions that students are required to ask need to be modeled and practiced prior to doing the activity.

Total physical response.

Before the class begins, develop a series of commands. First have students listen and watch as you demonstrate the commands. Next ask students to listen and demonstrate the commands as you call them out. After students are familiar with this activity, they can demonstrate the commands given by student volunteers. Practice can also be done in pairs in which one student calls the command series while the other student does the action.

Language experience.

In Language experience, the class generates a story that you write on the board. The students copy the story. Students can then practice reading in pairs or in small groups. As a follow-up activity, have students cut up their sentences, scramble them, and then reorder them.

CLOZE activity.

Photocopy the story but leave out key words. Have students complete the story. This activity can be made easier for lower students if the deleted key words are listed in random order on another piece of paper.

Cooperative learning techniques.

Roundtable: Divide the class into small groups of threes or fours. Give each group one copy of one practice activity and one pencil. Make sure all other pencils are put away. Model with one group before starting the activity. As the class watches, write or circle one answer. Pass the paper and pencil to the student on your right and have that student write or circle another answer. Continue having students fill in the paper and passing it on to the right. Do this until the entire activity is completed.

Line-up: Have students line up based on a question you ask or an order you give. For example, ask students to line up by alphabetical order of their last name, date of birth, etc. Most line-up activities can all be turned into graphing activities by having students graph the class line-up.

Pair dictation.

Have students dictate sentences from the text to their partners. Ask them to check their work by comparing it with the text after they finish.

Question grids.

Have students make question grids. Use this opportunity to introduce the words *column* and *row*. Model on the board by drawing a large grid. Say, "*Make 2 columns and 5 rows.*" Point to a column and a row.

Tell students to write *Name* at the top of one column and the question at the top of the second column. Then tell students to ask five classmates the same question and write their responses on the grid. The teacher should also mingle among the students to ask the same questions as well as to give help to students as needed.

Sample Grid

Name	Where do you live?

Tape dictation.

The purpose of tape dictation is to help students learn to listen to natural speech. This activity should be done only with material students have already studied. It is a good idea to let students study the passage in the text one time before starting the activity.

Students listen to one sentence at a time on the tape and write it. The line can be played as many times as necessary for students to feel comfortable. After the entire passage or dialog is completed, students should self-check their spelling and comprehension by referring to the text.

Disappearing conversation.

Have a student (or a few students) copy a dialog from the text on the board. Ask the class to read the conversation as you point to each word. Then erase the first line of the dialog and have the class read the conversation as you point. (Point to the erased line of the conversation as if it were there.) Continue this way until the entire conversation is erased.

Focused listening.

Focused listening is a technique in which the students are asked to listen for specific information. All of the opening activities lend themselves to this technique. Follow the steps given below.

1. Identify what you would like the students to listen for.
2. Play the tape.
3. Ask the students what they heard.
4. Write their responses on the board.
5. Ask a question. Replay the tape until the majority of students can identify the information asked for.

Unit	Culture Notes
1	**Introductions:** Discuss how students introduce each other in their native cultures.
2	**Families:** Discuss family names. How do people from the different cultures in your class address family members? Do they call them by first name, by family relationship, and so on?
3	**Food:** Discuss food items. Which food items are found in their country that are not found here? **Shopping:** Do they comparison shop in their countries? Do they bargain for food stuffs? Do they shop in supermarkets or open-air markets?
4	**Male/female roles:** Who does the shopping in their culture? Who does the chores? **Housing**: How does housing here differ from their countries? Do people rent or buy? How do they occupy the house? How many families typically live in one house? How large are typical houses?
5	**Shopping:** Discuss clothing sizes and gift giving: How do students from various countries figure out sizes? What sizes do they use? Where are shopping items displayed? in open-air markets, department stores, boutiques, and so on? How are items exchanged or brought back for return in various cultures? **Dates:** Discuss how various cultures write dates. Compare them to the US system of month/day/year. **Clothing:** Discuss formal versus informal clothing and what is appropriate clothing for celebrations, and so on.
6	**Sales:** How do students from different cultures feel about sales? Do they have yard sales, swap meets, and so on? How do they feel about used items that can be purchased in a thrift store or yard sale? **Household furniture:** What types of furniture are used in different types of cultures: for example beds, futons, hammocks, and so on. **Colors:** What is the significance of different colors: red, green, black, white, and so on?
7	**Emergencies:** How are medical emergencies handled in different cultures? Do other cultures call 911? How are emergency cases handled? How are accident emergencies handled in various cultures?
8	**Medicine:** What kinds of medicines are used for sickness? Do they have prescriptions and over-the-counter medicines? Who prescribes the medicine? When in the hospital, who is responsible for the day-to-day care: a nurse or the patient's family?

Unit	Culture Notes
9	**Travel:** How do people get to work? Do senior citizens get discounts on transportation/food? Who is responsible for senior citizens? Which is more common, private transportation or public? Do most people have cars? If so, how many cars do they have? **Signs:** Do other cultures use traffic signs? Are they used in the same ways or different ways? Are there universal traffic signs? What about signal lights? What are the different traffic patterns in different cultures?
10	**Occupations:** Are there similar degrees/licenses in other countries for certain jobs? What about certifying exams, such as for a CPA? **Careers:** Is there the notion of career ladders in other cultures? **Forms of address:** How do you address friends, colleagues, older people, and so on?
11	**Workplace behavior:** Are there rules for work breaks? What do people do on breaks? How many hours per day/week do people normally work? **Safety in the workplace:** Are there safety regulations in other cultures? Do people use/wear safety equipment while working? **Food:** Table manners with food and etiquette: Who starts to eat first? How much do you eat to be polite? What do you do when you want more food? What foods are typically eaten for breakfast, lunch, and dinner?
12	**Housing:** What does a typical house look like? How do people find housing? **Maintenance:** When renting, who takes care of problems in the house/apartment?
13	**Banks:** Are there banks in your culture? How do people save money? Where do people keep money? How do people send money? **Post Office:** In US money, what would be the cost for a local stamp; for an international stamp? Are post offices the same or different from this country? How are envelopes addressed? **Weather:** How do people dress for different weather? Is there a certain time when winter/summer clothing is worn? When is it appropriate to wear sandals, no tie, and so on?
14	**Generations:** Are there problems between the generations? Are there culture gaps/westernization problems? What types of chores are children expected to do? What are they not expected to do? When are girls allowed to wear makeup, style/perm their hair, and so on.
15	**Celebrations:** What types of holidays are celebrated in different countries? Talk about the different calendars: solar/lunar. Which calendar predominates? Why? **Food:** What types of food are made only for celebrations?

CASAS Life Skills Competencies Correlation for *English Extra*

Unit	Competency Number	Competency
All	0.1.2 0.1.3 0.1.4	Use language for informational purposes Use language to influence or persuade; request Use language in general social situations
1	0.1.5 0.2.1 0.2.2	Use appropriate classroom behavior Respond appropriately to personal information questions Complete personal information form
2	0.2.1 0.2.4 1.4.1 2.2.1 2.3.1 2.3.2	Respond appropriately to personal information questions Converse about daily activities and interests Identify types of housing, household items Ask for, give, follow, clarify directions Interpret clock time Identify months of the year and days of the week
3	1.1.6 1.2.1 1.3.8 2.2.1	Count, convert, and use coins and currency Interpret ads, labels, charts to select goods Identify common food items Ask for, give, follow, clarify directions
4	0.1.6 1.4.1 2.2.1 8.2.3	Clarify or request clarification Identify types of housing, households Ask for, give, clarify directions Recognize/demonstrate household tasks
5	1.1.9 1.2.2 1.3.3 1.3.9	Interpret clothing sizes Comparison shop: price, quality Use various methods to buy goods, services Identify common articles of clothing
6	1.2.1 2.2.1 2.2.5	Interpret ads, labels, charts to select goods Ask for, give, follow, clarify directions Use maps relating to travel needs
7	2.1.2 2.3.3 2.5.1 3.1.1 3.1.3	Identify emergency numbers, place calls Interpret information about weather conditions Locate emergency help agencies, low-cost legal aid Describe symptoms, parts of the body Identify appropriate health care services
8	3.1.1 3.3.1 3.5.9	Describe symptoms, parts of the body Identify and use necessary medications Practice physical well-being

Unit	Competency Number	Competency
9	2.2.1	Ask for, give, follow, clarify directions
	2.2.2	Recognize and use signs related to transportation
	2.2.4	Interpret transportation schedules and fares
	2.2.5	Use maps relating to travel needs
10	0.2.3	Interpret or write a note, invitation, or letter
	4.1.2	Interpret job applications, résumés, and so on
	4.1.3	Identify and use information in job ads
	4.1.6	Interpret work-related vocabulary
	4.1.8	Identify skills and education for various jobs
11	4.1.6	Interpret work-related vocabulary
	4.3.1	Interpret workplace safety signs
	4.5.1	Identify common tools, equipment, machines
12	1.4.1	Identify types of housing, household items
	1.4.2	Select housing, interpret classified ads
	1.4.7	Communicate housing problems
13	1.8.1	Demonstrate the use of checking, savings accounts
	1.8.2	Interpret procedures and forms for banking account
	2.4.4	Purchase stamps and other postal items, services
	2.4.6	Interpret a postal money order form
14	0.1.6	Clarify or request clarification
	2.1.7	Take, leave phone messages, use answering machines
	3.1.1	Describe symptoms, parts of the body
	5.1.6	Communicate one's opinions on a current issue
15	1.3.8	Identify common food items
	2.7.1	Interpret information about holidays
	8.1.1	Recognize/demonstrate hygiene and grooming skills

SCANS Competencies

SCANS competencies can be included in every unit by the following activities:

1) Resources: Students know how to allocate time, money, materials, space, and staff.

Time:

In activities which call for group or pair work, give each group or pair time limits on completing the activities. Leave it up to each group how to structure that time to finish the activity.

Materials:

When activities call for handouts, cutouts, and so on, give each group or pair a list of the materials needed for the activity. Have the students decide where to get the materials and who will get them.

Space:

When students are divided into groups or pairs, have them decide where the groups should meet. Encourage students to think about the layout of the room. Show students (initially) how to place their desks in convenient groups.

Staff:

In group or pair activities, show students how to include all members of the group. Praise examples of successful group behavior. Encourage other groups to follow good group behaviors.

2) Interpersonal Skill: Students can work in teams, teach others, serve customers, lead, negotiate, and work well with people from culturally diverse backgrounds.

Work in teams:

Divide students into regular teams and have them develop a team name. Have each team laminate a team folder in which to keep their written work.

Teach others:

When a student has been absent from class, have that student pair up with another student who was in attendance who can explain any necessary items that the absent student needs to complete. When a student is new to the class, assign a student to orient the new student to classroom procedures and policies.

Lead:

Have each student in a team take a turn being the team manager.

Negotiate:

Do a daily assessment of the class. Find out what students liked and did not like about each class. Encourage positive negotiation to develop classroom change. Daily assessment can include *yes/no* questions. Students either answer on a slip of paper or by putting their thumbs up for *yes* or down for *no*.

Work well with people from culturally diverse groups:

Encourage students to sit with partners from different cultures during pair and group work.

3) Information: Students can acquire and evaluate data, organize, and maintain files, interpret and communicate, and use computers to process information.

Every unit consists of an interview activity of some sort. After the interview activity is over, have the class compile the information about the class into a class graph and or a chart. This activity works particularly well with the following pages:

Unit 1, pages 8–9
Unit 2, pages 15, 19, 21
Unit 3, pages 25, 29
Unit 4, pages 38, 44–45
Unit 5, page 53
Unit 6, pages 62–63
Unit 8, page 94
Unit 9, pages 98, 99, 101,
Unit 10, pages 109, 113
Unit 11, pages 125, 128, 131
Unit 12, pages 137–138; 143
Unit 13, pages 136, 155
Unit 14, pages 159–160
Unit 15, pages 169–170, 174

4) Systems: Students understand social, organizational, and technological systems; they can monitor and correct performance; and they can design or improve systems.

Have students keep track of their performance on the last page of every unit, **I Can Do This!** Have students keep a running list of what they have learned and what they have missed. Encourage students to get help from other students in the group.

5) Technology: Students can select equipment and tools, apply technology to specific tasks, and maintain and troubleshoot equipment.

Use tape recorders, staplers, overhead projectors to complete the various assignments. Assign different groups of students to operate different types of equipment. For example, there are numerous places in each chapter where a tape is suggested. Each week assign a different group responsibility for running the tape player.

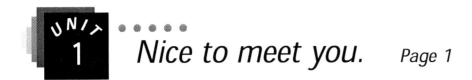

Nice to meet you. *Page 1*

Presentation.

For general suggestions about how to use this page refer to the Introduction. Always ask the general questions about the illustration before moving on to the more specific questions suggested for each unit. (See specific questions for this unit below.)

For most beginning students:

First demonstrate the command *point to* by pointing to the old man in the illustration. (Use a transparency, if available; if not, use the text.)

Is he old or young? *old*

(Next point to the youngest man.) Is he old or young*? young*

(Point to the third man.) Is he old or young? This question should promote a discussion about age.)

For low beginning students:

Are they all old? *No.*

Are they all wearing long pants? *No.*

Are they students or teachers*? students*

Are they in school or at home? *in school*

For more advanced students:

Who is old*? Van is.*

Who is young? *Bic is.*

What are they doing? *shaking hands*

Why? *They are meeting for the first time.*

How do you think they feel*? (Answers will vary: nervous, timid, happy, etc.)*

You may wish to find out the country of origin of students in your room. Make a class chart on the board with the two headings shown. As students name their country of origin try to elicit ways that people there greet each other when introduced.

Example:	**Country**	**Greeting**
	USA	Shake hands
	Korea	Bow

Listen and read.

Follow the presentation and practice directions in the Introduction. Point to each speech balloon as you read the dialog aloud. Write the name of each character on the board. Then have students guess each character's country of origin. Next read the dialog again and encourage students to read along with you silently or orally.

Follow-up activities.

Introduce this activity by modeling for students. Have a student stand up. Introduce yourself to the student by shaking hands and saying, "*Hi!* (_____*'s*) *my name. Nice to meet you.*" Encourage the student to respond, "*I'm* (name). *Pleased to meet you, too.*"

Repeat this procedure with four more students. Then ask students to introduce themselves to at least five students in the class. Encourage alternate greetings: *Hello, Hey, Hi.*

How are you?   Page 2

Follow the tape or read aloud the tapescript on page 181 in the back of the student book.

My name is . . . .   Page 3

Follow the tape or read aloud the introductions in the book.

Small group practice.

Divide students into small groups of 5 or 6. Have them do the practice page in their group by each student introducing him/herself to the other members of the group.

Have students complete the writing section on page 3 in their small groups. Encourage group members to help each other. Have group members read their "write" activity to each other. Mingle through the classroom to answer questions of individual students and to help lower-level ones progress.

Follow-up activity.

Discuss naming systems in other countries. For example in Korea the written order is last name, first name, and then middle name. There are always three parts to every name.

In Latin America people often have longer names that contain names from their mother's side of the family as well as from their father's side.

Make a master list on the board that might look something like this:

Country	Sample name
United States	First name, middle name, last name
Korea	Last name, first name, middle name
Mexico	First name, father's last name, (followed by *de* for *of)*, mother's maiden last name)

How are you feeling?   Page 4

Students were introduced to words for positive/good feelings on page 2. On this page, they are introduced to words for more negative feelings (*sad, bored, sick,* etc.). Contrast the happy smiles shown on the faces on page 2 with expressions on the faces of the people on this page.

Follow the tape or read aloud the tapescript on page 181.

Review the letters of the alphabet in upper and lowercase letters. Give help as needed to students who are having difficulty forming letters. If possible, display classroom charts or cards that show the alphabet, both in manuscript and cursive forms.

Assign workbook pages 1 and 2.

Workbook answers:

Page 1

a. happy	d. fine	g. angry	j. sick
b. sad	e. good	h. tired	k. great
c. upset	f. so-so	i. bored	

Page 2

A. Students should write the alphabet in upper and lowercase letters.
B. Students should write the missing letters.

Do you remember?   Page 5 (Review)

If possible, make a transparency of this page. Read each letter and have the students read after you.

Language note:

Spanish speakers are easily confused by our English vowel names. Pronounce the vowels *a, e,* and *i* very carefully as well as the letters *y, g,* and *h.*

Play the tape (Part 1) or read the tapescript in the back of the book. Ask students to circle each letter they hear.

Answers: Part 1

1. v	2. e	3. e	4. s	5. g	6. s	7. a	8. n	9. y

Spell the following words letter by letter and have the class guess each word. Then write the words on the board for the class to compare them and check their work.

teacher, student, upset, sad, happy, first, name, last

Read each number aloud and have the students repeat them.

Play the tape (Part 2) or read the tapescript in the back of the book. Have students circle the number they hear.

Answers: Part 2

1. 13	2. 22	3. 12	4. 4	5. 6	6. 29	7. 28	8. 30	9. 17

Follow-up activity.

Say random numbers and have students write them. Then write the numbers on the board for the class to check. (Example: 131, 20, 30, 987, 1001, 364, 533, 15, 70)

Play the tape (Part 3) or read the tapescript on page 181 and have students write in the letters over the correct numbers. Have them read the completed words.

Answer: Part 3

great student

Follow-up activity.

Divide students into groups and show them how to make up their own number puzzles. Distribute student-made number puzzles to the class. Ask each group to dictate the letters that go over the numbers.

Assign workbook page 3.

Workbook answers:
    Part 3:   a. 10, 14, 18, 20   b. 22, 26, 30   c. 9, 15, 21

This is our classroom.   Page 6 (Vocabulary)

Follow the general directions described in the Introduction for a vocabulary page.

Use the tape or read the tapescript on page 182.

Follow-up activity.

Have students label the items in your classroom. Divide the students into small groups. Give each group a list of a few words from page 6 along with some index cards and tape. Have them write one word on each card, find that object in the room, and tape the card to it. Elicit from students other items in the classroom not listed on page 6 and label those as well.

Is this a clock ?   Page 7 (Vocabulary reinforcement)

Follow the tape or read the tapescript on page 182.

Answers:
    1. no 2. yes 3. yes 4. yes 5. no 6. yes 7. no 8. yes 9. no 10. no 11. yes 12. no

Practice.

Have students find partners, then ask and answer the two types of questions listed on page 7: *Is this a _____ ? What's this?* First model the activity before asking students to practice. Tell students to ask each other questions about the items in your classroom.

Assign workbook page 4.

Answers:

a. computer	d. screen	g. board	j. map
b. wheelchair	e. flag	h. clock	k. projector
c. calculator	f. calendar	i. pencil sharpener	l. bookcase

Here is your identification card.   Page 8

Presentation.

If possible, make an overhead transparency of the page. Have students look at both José's and Sue's School Identification cards at the top of the page. Use TPR and first ask students to point to each section of the ID card. Then ask students: *Is this José's card or Sue's card?* (Point to José's card). *In what city does José live? What is his street address? What is his zip code? What is his telephone number? Is 619 his zip code or area code?*

Ask the same questions for Sue's card.

Model how to fill in the identification card by writing your information on a transparency in the space provided. Be sure to show students the correct format for both their address and telephone number.

Follow-up activity.

Copy another school identification form. Have students interview each other and fill in the form for their partner. First ask a student the following questions: *What is your name? What is your address? What is your telephone number?* Also say, *Could you spell that, please?* and *Please repeat that.*

Ask your classmates.

On the board, write the following:

What is your first name?   How do you spell that, please?
What is your last name?   How do you spell that, please?

Model the activity by asking five students for their first name and last name and writing their names on a transparency. Then have students mingle, ask 5 classmates the question, and fill in the information.

Male? Female?   Page 9

If possible, make a transparency of the page. Follow the tape or tapescript on page 182.

Write about you.

Model how to fill in the form by doing it on a transparency or copy the information shown on the form on the board, then write in your information. Discuss the meaning of each term used on the form.

> **Culture notes:**
> 1. Make sure students understand the difference between signing and printing their names.
> 2. Some students may be reluctant to indicate they are divorced. Give students options.

Count your classmates.   Page 10

This is best done as a whole class activity. Make a transparency of the page. Have students count the total number of students in the class. Place the total number on the transparency. Next, have all the single students stand up. (Once again, divorced or widowed students may wish to stand with the singles.) Continue until all students have stood and have been counted in one category or the other. Show students how to add up the numbers to equal the total.

Have students complete the bar graph. Ask them to first copy the numbers for single, married, and divorced students on the left. Show students how to color in squares for the different numbers. If crayons are available, students can use different colors for each graph.

Assign workbook page 5.

Note: Review the meaning of any words on the form that need reinforcement.

Answers:
1. d   2. i   3.a   4. b   5.c   6. h   7.f   8. e   9.g

Review. Page 11

Follow the tape or read the tapescript and have students circle each correct answer.

Listen and circle.

Answers:
1. b   2. a   3. b   4. a

Find the picture and write the word.

In pairs or small groups have students fill in the answers.

Answers:			
1. clock	4. bookcase	7. calculator	10. calendar
2. board	5. computer	8. flag	11. map
3. pencil sharpener	6. projector	9. screen	12. wheelchair

Assign workbook page 6.

This page can be used to start students working on student produced publications. If possible, make a transparency of the page. Guide students to write the information asked for in the various sections. Have students pair off and read their stories to each other. Model this by using your own story. If there is a computer available in the class or if there is a computer lab, have students word process their stories. Pairs may check for beginning and end punctuation. Print the stories out and display them in the class. You may prefer to develop a class book for each student of all finished stories. If a camera is available, pictures of students can be taken and placed with individual stories.

I can do this! Page 12

Follow the general directions in the Introduction.

Assign the Crossword Puzzle and Wordsearch, Workbook pages 7 and 8.

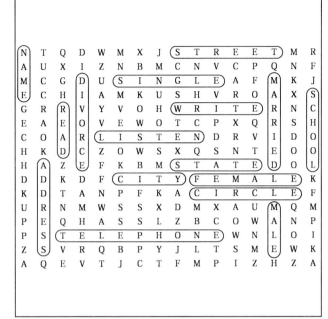

There is no school on Saturday. Page 13

Presentation.

For general suggestions about how to use this page refer to the Introduction. Always ask the general questions about the illustration before moving on to the more specific questions suggested for each unit. (See specific questions for this unit below.)

For most beginning students:

Are there 4 or 5 people? *5*
Are they eating or studying? *eating*
Is it morning or night? *morning*
Are they eating rice or bread? *rice*
Are they friends or family? *family*

For low beginning students:

Are there 5 people? *Yes*
Are they a family? *Yes*
Are they at school? *No, they are at home.*
Are they eating rice? *Yes*
Is it morning or night? (Indicate the window showing the day.) *morning*

For more advanced students:

How many people are there? *5*

Where are they? *at home*
What are Kim, Charlie, May, and Grandpa doing? *eating*
Point to the grandfather.
Point to the daughter.
Circle the mother.

Follow the Introduction. Then play the tape or use the tapescript.

Have students answer the following questions as a whole class:

Can Bic go to school today? *No. He needs to work.*

Can Grandpa go to school today? (Point to the title that says there is no school.) *No.*

Why does Grandpa need Bic to go to school? *Perhaps school is too far from home and Grandpa needs Bic to drive him.*

Follow-up activity.

Have a discussion about morning meals. Point to the picture and ask, "What are they eating? Do you eat rice for breakfast? What do you eat in the morning?" Talk about eating practices.

What do you do on Saturdays?   Page 14

Write these words on the board: *shop, rest, dance, go to school, go to work, exercise.* Point to each word and have students read it. After you find out which words they seem to understand, mime for them the ones they do not.

Next list the days of the week on the board; have students read each one aloud. Ask them, *"What is today?"* Point to each day of the week and ask in a questioning way, *"school?"* Students should answer *Yes* on the days that they go to school. For Saturday and Sunday they most likely will answer *No.* (**Note:** If your school has Saturday school, then use Sunday instead of Saturday.) Then write *shop?* See if some students answers, *"Yes."* Go through each of the activities previously covered.

Using the transparency, ask the students the questions, then have the students read them aloud. Circle your own answers and have students circle their answers. Then pair students and have them practice asking a partner each question.

Follow-up activity.
Cooperative learning activity corners:

Post a leisure activity in three corners of the room. In the fourth corner post "other." Have students move to the corner that best describes their Saturday activity. If they do not engage in one of the three activities posted, they should go to the "other" corner. Ask those in the "other" corner what they actually do. List their activities on the board.

Look at the week.   Page 15

Follow the tape or read the tapescript on page 182. Then have students practice the third conversation (shown with the blanks). Use today's date and model how students should practice asking questions with each of the words in the practice activity. Then have students practice asking and answering the question about today with their partner.

Example: *Today is Monday. Do you go to school on Monday? Yes, I do./ No, I don't. I work on Monday.*

Follow-up activity.

Find someone who . . .

_____ goes to work on Saturdays.

_____ goes to school on Fridays.

_____ exercises on Tuesdays.

_____ shops on Mondays.

_____ rests on Sundays.

_____ dances on Saturdays.

Process.

Students mingle with classmates and ask, *Do you _____?"* (. . . *go to school, exercise, shop, rest, dance*)

When a classmate answers *"Yes,"* the inquisitor should write the classmate's name in the space. They may only use a name one time in one space. The objective is to fill in each space with a different name.

Assign workbook pages 9 and 10.

Workbook answers:

Page 9. Answers will vary.

a. Do you rest on Saturdays?	Yes, I do rest on Saturdays.
	No, I don't. I _____ on Saturdays.
b. Do you exercise on Saturdays?	Yes, I do. I exercise on Saturdays.
	No, I don't. I _____ on Saturdays.
c. Do you go to work on Saturdays?	Yes, I do. I go to work on Saturdays.
	No, I don't. I _____ on Saturdays.
d. Do you go to school on Saturdays?	Yes, I do. I go to school on Saturdays.
	No, I don't. I ____ on Saturdays.

Review.   Page 16

Follow the tape or read the tapescript.

Write about *you*.

Have students fill in what they do on Fridays, Saturdays, and Sundays.

Follow-up activity.

Do a question grid activity with 4 columns and the headings: Name, Friday, Saturday, Sunday. Add 6 rows.

Ask your classmates.   Page 17

Have students write the names of the days of the week on the lines. Model this activity by doing it on the transparency first.

Next write the question, *"What day do you _____?"* One at a time, put each of the activities in the space. Have students practice reading the question two or three times.

Have students mingle and ask classmates the questions. Encourage students to try to fill in their charts completely.

What time is it?   Page 18

Follow the tape or read the tapescript.

Answers: Listen and check the time you hear.

   1. b   2. b   3. a   4. a   5. b   6. b

Assign workbook page 11.

Follow-up activity.

Ask students to listen and then write each time as you read it aloud. Divide the class into pairs. Have students write 5 different units of time and then dictate the units of time to their partner.

    7:15   3:33   2:15   8:30   1:45   12:00 noon

Please turn on the lamp.   Page 19

Listen and point.

Follow the tape or read the tapescript on page 183. Then call students' attention to the picture and ask: *Where is the lamp? (It's on the small table.)* Repeat the same procedure with each of the items.

Practice.

Write the words *on, next to, above,* and *under* on the board as they appear on the page. Read each word aloud. Then read each sentence from the student book and ask students to repeat it after you. Have students practice asking partners *Where* questions.

Assign workbook pages 12 and 13.

This is the Castro Family.   Page 20

Presentation.

Go over the family relationships. Have students listen to the story on the tape or use the tapescript. Read the story aloud and have students follow along in their books. Then have the students read aloud after you. Next, divide the class into pairs and have them draw a line to show the relationships of the family members (Ricardo's wife: Carmen).

Answers:

    1. d   2. f   3. b   4. a (e)   5. c   6. g   7. e   8. h

Follow-up activity.

Divide students into groups of 6-8 students. Write the following on the board: *My name is _____. I am the father.*

Tell students to create an imaginary family. They should include each person's name and tell the person's relationship to the family. Other vocabulary words the students may want to include are *cousin, aunt, uncle, niece, nephew.*

After the groups have created their fictional families, they can play a guessing game. One student in a group begins by saying, *"My name is _____."* Other students in the class must try to get as much information as possible by asking questions. Write these question types on the board. (Examples: *"Are you the uncle? Are you _____ years old?"*

Optional review.

Pair Dictation: In pairs have students dictate the story in the text to their partners, sentence by sentence. Check their work. Then ask them to change partners and repeat the dictation.

I'm her brother. She's my sister. Page 21

Make a transparency. Have students fill in the blanks.

Answers:					
1. mother	2. daughter	3. mother	4. wife	5. sister	6. son

Write the answers on the transparency and have students check their work.

Assign workbook page 14.

Point to each word in the box and have students read each word aloud. Model the activity by filling in the boxes with information about your family.

Help students evaluate their information from the grid.

Follow-up activity.

Student-produced publications can be introduced at this time. To provide a model for students, write a short paragraph about your family. Photocopy it and hand out copies to the class. Ask students to use their charts to write a story about their family. If there is a computer available in the class or if there is a computer lab, have students word process their stories. Print these out for display or develop a class book for each student of the finished stories. If you wish, encourage students to bring in photos of their family to include with their stories. If a scanner is available, photos can be scanned and placed electronically with the students' stories. If no scanner is available, have students photocopy the photos and put the copies on/with their stories.

Review. Page 22

Use the tape if it is available. Have students complete the page.

Answers: Write the letter.

    1. f   2. b   3. g   4. d   5. c   6. f & e

Answers: Write the word.

    1. She   2. They 3. They 4. They 5. It

It's time to go.   Page 23

Ask students to look only at the picture. Ask them the following questions:

1. How many people are there?   3. What is under the table?
2. What are they doing?

Then follow the tape or use the tapescript. Have students complete the page.

Follow-up activity.

Use the dialog to have students focus their listening and take dictation. Refer to the Introduction for detailed instructions.

I can do this!   Page 24

Follow the general directions in the Introduction.

Assign the Crossword Puzzle and Wordsearch, Workbook pages 15 and 16.

 UNIT 2 *Crossword Puzzle*

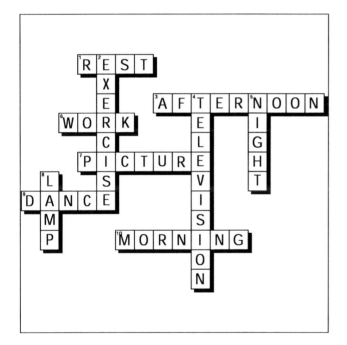

 UNIT 2 *Wordsearch*

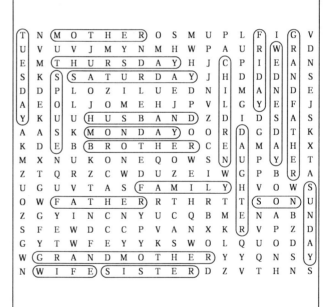

Can we buy some ice cream? *Page 25*

Presentation.

For general suggestions about how to use this page refer to the Introduction. Always ask the general questions about the illustration before moving on to the more specific questions suggested for each unit. (See specific questions for this unit below.)

For most beginning students:

Are there 2 or 3 people working at the store? *2*

Are the customers eating or shopping? *shopping*

Are they in a grocery store or a school? *grocery store*

Are there 5 or 6 aisles? *5*

For low beginning students:

Are there 5 people working? *No, there are two.*

Are the customers shopping? *Yes.*

Are they at school? *No, they are in a grocery store (supermarket).*

Are there five aisles? *Yes*

For more advanced students:

How many people are working? *two people*

Where are they? *at a grocery store*

What are the customers doing? *They are shopping.*

How many aisles are there? *5*

Are there any sales today? *Yes.*

Where is the girl in a wheelchair? *at the checkout counter*

Follow-up activity.

Talk about shopping habits. Find out how many people shop monthly, weekly, daily. Find out what supermarket the students use. Make a bar graph to show the names of stores where students shop and the number of students who shop at the stores listed. Then point to each section of the supermarket pictured. Ask students what the areas are called (aisles). Find out if any students work in a supermarket.

Optional follow-up activity.

The next day of class, have a tape dictation. See the Introduction for details.

Where's the ice cream?   Page 26

Listen and read.

Put the words *aisle, frozen foods, ice cream,* and *over there* on the board. As you point to each word, have students read it. Find out which words students understand, then mime those they do not know.

Play the tape or read the tapescript and have students follow along. Have students practice the conversation in pairs. Do a "disappearing conversation" activity. (See the Introduction.)

Listen, find the picture, and read the word.

Run your finger along the first row of food objects. Tell students that things as well as people can be in a line or row. Compare the lines of food with the lines of people at the check-out counters shown on the previous page. Then point to each picture on a transparency or in a student book as you say the word. Have students repeat each word after you.

Then follow the tape or tapescript and the procedure for presenting and discussing the unit.

Follow-up activities.

For vocabulary practice and reinforcement, have students make food index cards.

First, photocopy the page. Give each student 20 index cards, a glue stick, and scissors. Write the directions shown below on the board.

1. Cut out each picture.
2. Glue the picture on the index card.
3. Write the word for each picture on the back.
4. Throw away your scraps.
5. Put the glue stick and scissors away.
6. Ask me for a rubber band.
7. Practice reading and saying the words on your cards.

Do a total physical response activity at this time. (See the Introduction for details.) Have students save their word cards to use with the next lesson.

Use workbook page 17. With the class, read aloud the jazz chants. You may wish to use a ruler or a stick to beat out the rhythm as the words are read. You may also choose a volunteer to "keep the beat."

Where are the oranges?   Page 27

Listen, read, and practice with your partner.

Make a transparency of the page, if possible. Have students follow along with you.

Point to the categories, one at a time. Have students read after you as you say, "*Fruits*" (pause) "*Vegetables*." Next point to the specific items in each category and have students read after you.

Discuss any new words. Write the categories on the board and have students close their books. Have students take out the word cards that they made to go along with page 26 and divide them up by category.

Compare the two conversations on pages 26 and 27. Notice that on page 27 categories are used, additional items are listed, and aisle locations of items are mentioned. Then have students practice the conversation by changing both the items and the categories (Example: *"Where is beef?/" "It's in aisle 4 with Meats, Poultry,* and *Fish."*). Students may use either or both conversational models.

Listen and read the food words.

Follow the tape or use the tapescript.

Follow-up activities.

Have students add to their food cards by making more cards with the additional vocabulary. Write the words *alphabetical order* on the board. Explain what it means. Say, "*A, B, C*" as you write *ABC order* on the board.

Have students order their cards by having one group write all the A words on the board, another group the B words, and so on.

Assign workbook page 18.

Workbook answers:

Page 18

1. bananas	5. chicken	9. salt	13. noodles
2. cabbage	6. pork	10. rice	14. broccoli
3. bread	7. sugar	11. cake	15. fish
4. oranges	8. coffee	12. peaches	16. cookies

Write. Use a transparency or write the sentence at the bottom of page 27 on the board with blanks, as shown. Model how to write in answers by using your own likes and dislikes.

Follow-up activity.

Do the question grid activity found in the Introduction with a grid of 3 columns for <u>Name, likes, doesn't like</u>. Add 6 rows.

Review.   Page 28

Review the vocabulary words with the class. Follow the tape or tapescript.

Answers:

    1. b   2. b   3. a   4. c   5. c

Review.   Page 29

Follow the tape or tapescript.

Answers:

1. yes	3. no	5. yes	7. yes	9. no	11. yes
2. no	4. yes	6. no	8. no	10. no	12. yes

Note: For plural words such as *cookies, noodles,* and *potatoes,* make sure the students use *these* in place of *this* and *are* in place of *is.*

Model the first practice by asking the class a few *Yes/No* questions. Students should then practice the questions in pairs using their word cards. Next introduce *What* questions by modeling a few. Have students practice asking and answering these questions by using their word cards.

Assign workbook page 19.

Publish students' completed pages by posting them on the wall or by copying them for each member of the class.

Follow-up activity.

Which is different? In this activity students practice making statements while reviewing spelling and vocabulary. Dictate a series of three words—two that have a connection and one that does not. For example, *flour, sugar, orange.* Ask students to write the three words.

Then ask them which one is different in some way. If they say *orange,* for example, ask, *Why?* They may say that flour and sugar are baking goods and an orange is a fruit. Help them to express this in a sentence. Continue with the following series of words.

1. cabbage, broccoli, butter (Cabbage and broccoli are vegetables and butter is a dairy product.)
2. milk, butter, soda (Milk and butter are dairy products and soda is a beverage.)
3. chicken, pork, bread (Chicken and pork are meats and bread is a bakery product.)
4. bananas, peaches, beans (Bananas and peaches are fruits and beans are vegetables.)
5. soda, coffee, ice cream (Soda and coffee are beverages; ice cream is a frozen food.)

Assign workbook page 20.

Use the question grid process for this activity.

Follow-up activity.

Have students find out from their classmates what their favorite fruits, vegetables, and meats are. Then have the class make a bar graph.

Do you sell soda?　Page 30

If possible, make an overhead transparency of this page. Ask students to tell you what they can about the picture. Make sure that students understand that the customers are asking questions about what the store sells.

Review the 40 vocabulary words and make sure all students understand the meaning of each one. Have students take out their word cards to see which words they have cards for and which they need to make. You can have students add more cards by drawing pictures of the missing items or by finding pictures of items in magazines.

Write *supermarket* on the board. Ask students what other types of stores there are. With your encouragement, brainstorm a list with the class. (Possible answers: *department store, pharmacy, butcher shop, stationary shop,* and so on.) Have students divide objects based on store types.

I like cookies! I like cake!　Page 31

Presentation.

Divide students into small groups. Have each group create a store. (Help students by asking questions, such as *What is the name of the store? What type of store is it? department store, food store, specialty shop (butcher, stationary, etc.) What items do you sell?* (Pull out word cards for the items and have students put these items in aisles.) Have groups rotate from store to store and find out what each store sells.

Have students fill in the spaces of the two writing activities.

Follow-up activities.

Review the food items on the page. Then have students make a list of foods they like and foods they do not like. Ask students to pair off. They should find out what foods they have in common and make a list. If partners have nothing in common, have students search for partners with whom they do have something in common.

Have students play the *I am going to the market* game. Ask students to place chairs in a large circle. The first person says, "*I am going to the market to buy* and names one item. Each player thereafter repeats any items mentioned and adds one more. The teacher finishes the list by being the last player.

How much does it cost?   Page 32

Follow the tape or use the tapescript.

How much money do you have?   Page 33

Review the coins and dollars. Follow the tape or use the tapescript.

Follow-up activity.

Money Dictation: Dictate the prices below and have students write them. Next ask them to form pairs. Have each person write 5 prices, then dictate the prices to a partner.

Assign workbook pages 21 and 22.

Answers:					
Page 21					
1. $3.99	2. $3.98	3. $5.00	4. $3.88	5. $3.00	
Answers:					
Page 22					
1. $.24	2. $.18	3. $1.10	4. $3.24	5. $11.13	6. $1.02

Follow-up activities.

Word problems. Dictate or photocopy the following word problems and have students answer them.

1. You buy 2 pounds of cabbage that cost $.57 a pound, 6 pounds of bananas that cost 4 pounds for $1.00, and one bag of sugar for $1.57. What is the total price?_____
   (*Answer:* $4.21)
   You give the salesclerk $20.00. How much change do you get back? _____
   (*Answer:* $15.79)

2. You buy five pounds of flour for $2.59, 3 pounds of apples at $.29 a pound, and 2 pounds of meat at $1.29 a pound. What is your total price?   (*Answer:* $6.04)
   You give the salesclerk $10.00. How much do you get back?   (*Answer: $*3.96)

Which is the best buy?   Page 34

Have students circle the cheaper item.

> *Answers:*
>
> 1. a   2. a   3. b   4. b   5. b.   6. a   7. b.   8. b

Follow-up activity.

Ask students to tell why one price is better than the other.

> *Answers:*
>
> 1. The bread costs less.
> 2. A whole peach is better than a half peach.
> 3. Each pound is only $1.24.
> 4. Twenty-four cookies would be only $1.20.
> 5. Five pounds is $2.50.
> 6. The second pound is free.
> 7. Flour is less money.
> 8. Each head of lettuce is $.70.

Review.   Page 35

Follow the tape or use the tapescript for the first two activities. Have students circle the cor-rect answers for the best buy.

> *Answers:*
>
> *Circle the amount:*   1.b   2. c   3. a   4. c   5.c   6. a
>
> *Circle the best buy:*   1. b   2.b   3. b   4. a

I can do this!   Page 36

See the Introduction for instructions on ways of using this page.

Assign the Crossword Puzzle and Wordsearch, Workbook pages 23 and 24.

 UNIT 3 Crossword Puzzle

 UNIT 3 Wordsearch

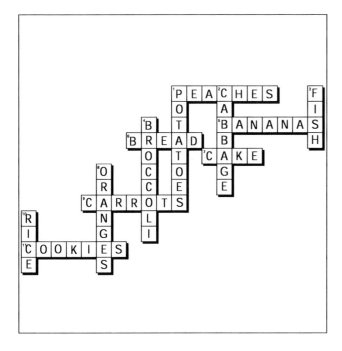

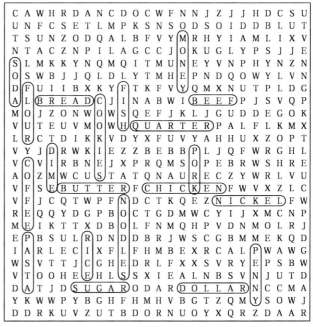

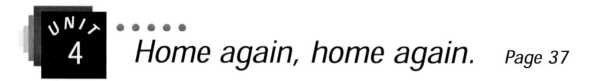

Home again, home again. *Page 37*

Presentation.

For general suggestions about how to use this page refer to the Introduction. Always ask the general questions about the illustration before moving on to the more specific questions suggested for each unit. (See specific questions for this unit below.)

For most beginning students:

Is this a kitchen or a bedroom? *kitchen*

Are there 3 or 4 people in the kitchen? *3*

Are they eating or unpacking the groceries? *unpacking the groceries*

Are the groceries on the sink or the table? *on the table*

Is the man in front of the shelf or in front of the stove? *in front of the shelf*

Is the refrigerator next to the cabinet or next to the stove? *next to the cabinet*

Are the curtains above the sink or above the refrigerator? *above the sink*

Is the sink between the stove and the refrigerator or between the man and the shelf? *between the stove and the refrigerator*

For low beginning students:

Is this a kitchen? *Yes.*

Are there 4 people? *No, there are only 3.*

Are they at school? *No, they are at home in the kitchen.*

Are they unpacking the groceries? *Yes.*

Are the groceries on the table? *Yes.*

Is the man in front of the stove? *No, he is in front of the shelf.*

Is the refrigerator next to the cabinets? *Yes.*

Are the curtains above the refrigerator? *No, they are above the sink.*

Is the sink between the man and the shelf? *No, it is between the stove and the refrigerator.*

For more advanced students:

How many people are in the picture? *3*

Where are they? *at home in the kitchen*

What are the they doing? *unpacking the groceries*

Where is the stove? *under the microwave oven*

Where is the microwave? *over the stove*

Where is the sink? *under the curtains (over the cabinets) (between the cabinets and curtains)*

Where are the curtains? *over the sink*

Where is the cabinet? *under the sink*

Where is the refrigerator? *between the sink and the shelf*

Where is the shelf? *next to the refrigerator*

Where are the groceries? *on the table and under the table*

They're unpacking the groceries.   Page 38

Presentation.

For general suggestions about how to use this page refer to the Introduction.

Write the missing words.

Read the paragraph aloud, pausing long enough for students to fill in each missing word. Then have one or more volunteers read their completed paragraph aloud.

Follow-up activities.

Ask students to tell you about the relationships of the people in the picture. What is the man (father) doing? What are the little girl and the mother doing? Who does the shopping in your family? If you wish, encourage students to discuss the various roles that members in their family carry out.

Optional follow-up activity.

The next class day give students a tape dictation. See the Introduction for details.

Assign Workbook page 25. Point to the word *cabinet.* Then point to the cabinet pictured with a 1 in the circle. Then say, "*2. floor.*" Most students should be able to complete the activity independently. Give help to students as needed.

Practice.

Review the food words in the left box. Review the phrases in the right box. Clarify the meaning of each phrase. Divide the class into small groups and have them discuss where they think each food item should go. Each group may have different answers.

Follow the tape or use the tapescript.

Rearrange the students into pairs. Have them practice the conversation.

Follow-up activity.

Have students divide the food cards that they made for Unit 3 according to where the food goes. Make a master grid on the board of the 7 locations and decide as a whole class where each item goes.

Assign workbook page 26. Answers will vary.

Want some help?   Page 39

Have students cover the story with a sheet of paper and look only at the picture. Write the words *cleaning house* on the board. Allow students to "talk" to each other about the picture. Encourage students to respond to questions. Restate their ideas in acceptable English and write their responses on the board. Read aloud what you have written. Continue until all of the following household chores have been written on the board:

mowing the lawn (cutting the grass)	cleaning the kitchen
doing the laundry	sweeping
hanging out the clothes	cleaning the upstairs bedroom
cleaning the bathroom	

Have students close their books. Do a focused listening activity. Follow the directions in the Introduction. Then ask students to open their books.

Listen and read.

Follow the tape or read the dialog and the paragraph about the Said family to the class.

Ask students to practice reading the story in pairs. Follow up with a tape dictation or a paired dictation. See directions in the Introduction.

What are the rooms in the house?   Page 40

Have students cover the **Listen and read** section with a piece of paper.

Write the words *my house* on the board. Allow students to "talk" to each other about the picture. Encourage students to respond to questions. Restate their ideas in acceptable English and write the words on the board. Read aloud what you have written.

Continue until all of the following words have been written on the board:

front yard	balcony/patio	living room
basement	kitchen	bathroom
back yard	dining room	bedroom

Follow the tape or read aloud **Listen and read.** Then ask students to write the missing words.

Answers:

1. bedrooms, living room, dining room, bathrooms, and kitchen
2. four.
3. two
4. basement
5. behind
6. next . . . kitchen

Follow-up activity.

Do a tape dictation or a paired dictation. See directions in the Introduction.

Assign workbook page 27. Tell students to refer to the pictures on pages 37 through 40 for the answers.

Answers:

    living room: chairs, picture, sofa, mirror, lamps, table, curtains, TV
    bedroom: chest, picture, bed, closet, TV, lamps, curtains
    bathroom: mirror, tub, cabinet, shower, sink
    kitchen: chairs, stove, microwave, stove, refrigerator, cabinet, table, sink

Who's doing what? Where?   Page 41

Follow the instructions given in the Introduction for the vocabulary pages.

Answers:

1. bedroom	4. dining room	7. laundry room
2. bathroom	5. kitchen	8. basement
3. living room	6. garage	9. yard

Practice. Page 42

Review the following: *Where is/are, He is/They are,* and *He's/She's.*

Students can create their own dialogs based on the reading on the previous page. Model a few sentences. Ask students to practice in pairs.

Follow-up activity.

Play a game of Scrambled Sentences. Photocopy the activity. Have students cut out each word. Then tell them to mix up or "scramble" the words on their desks. After they have done that, challenge them to put the words back into sentence order.

> *Possible answers:*
> 1. Grandpa Said is in the bedroom. He's reading a book.
> 2. Linda is in the laundry room. She's washing the clothes.
> 3. Ali is in the bedroom. He's making the bed.
> 4. Ibrahim is in the yard. He's hanging out the clothes.
> 5. Grandma is in the kitchen. She's cooking.

Assign workbook page 28.

> *Answers:*
> 1. Grandpa is reading a book.
> 2. Farima is sweeping the bathroom floor.
> 3. Mohammed is cleaning the bedroom.
> 4. Grandma is cooking in the kitchen.
> 5. Ibrahim is cutting the grass in the yard.
> 6. Linda is making the bed.

Use workbook page 29.

Do the jazz chant entitled *Cooking chicken in the kitchen* with the class. See the Introduction for specific instructions.

José's place. Page 43

Have students cover the **Listen and Read** section with a piece of paper.

Write the words *José's place* on the board. Allow students to "talk" to each other about the picture. Encourage students to respond to questions. Restate their ideas in acceptable English words, phrases, and sentences and write them on the board. Read what you have written. Continue until all the objects in *José's place* are on the board.

Follow the tape or use the tapescript.

Follow-up activity.

Have students close their books. Do a focused listening activity. See the Introduction.

Review.   Page 44

Follow the tape or use the tapescript.

Answers:				
Living Room:	1. sofa	2. TV	3. picture	4. table
Kitchen:	1. cabinet	2. microwave	3. refrigerator	4. stove
Bedroom:	1. bed	2. night stand	3. lamp	4. dresser
Bathroom:	1. sink	2. tub	3. shower	4. toilet

Follow-up activity.

This page can be used to work on student-produced publications. As a model write a short paragraph about your house. Photocopy it and hand it out to the class. Ask them to use it to write a story about their house. If there is a computer available in the class or if there is a computer lab, have students word process their stories. Print these out and display them or develop a class book for each student of all finished stories. Ask students to bring in a photo of their house to put with their story. If a scanner is available, scan the photos and place them with the students' stories. If no scanner is available, have students photocopy their photos and put them with their stories.

Today is Carmen's birthday.   Page 45

Allow students to "talk" to each other about the picture. Encourage students to respond to questions. Restate their ideas in acceptable English and write the words, phrases, or sentences on the board. Read aloud what you have written.

Have students read the text silently. Try to find out which words they don't understand and review them. A good technique is to show students how to underline unknown or difficult words. Then ask them to follow the same procedure.

Put students in pairs and have them answer the questions. Go over their answers as a whole group.

Answers:	
1. Carmen is having a birthday party.	4. She's 35 years old.
2. They are cleaning all the rooms.	5. Her husband and son are hanging balloons.
3. Her mother is.	

Follow-up activity.

List the countries your students come from on the board. Say, "Tell me about birthdays in your country." Try to elicit how birthdays in their country differ from a US birthday. Bring in a picture of a birthday party at your house and encourage students to bring in pictures of birthdays at their houses.

Balloons, balloons, balloons.   Page 46

Review the color words. Then review the numbers. Have students write in the answers.

Answers:					
1. 4 green	2. 5 blue	3. 2 purple	4. 4 orange	5. 3 yellow	5. 7 red

Do the jazz chant *Color My Balloon* on the bottom of **workbook page 29.**

Assign workbook page 30. Make sure students understand how to complete Part B (the interview section).

Counting the cookies.   Page 47

Follow the tape or read the dialog aloud. Review the names of food items in the 10 practice boxes. Divide students into pairs and have them practice the conversation. Remind students that the person whose speech balloon has a question mark should begin the conversation.

I can do this!   Page 47

See the Introduction for instructions on ways of using this page.

Assign the Crossword Puzzle and Wordsearch, Workbook pages 31 and 32.

Remind students to check off each word after they circle it. Give help to students who are having difficulty.

 UNIT 4 Crossword Puzzle

 UNIT 4 Wordsearch

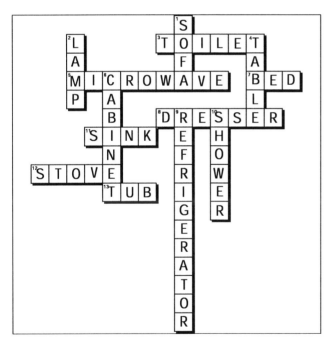

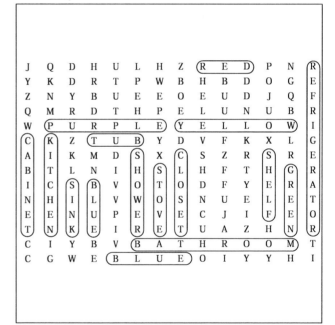

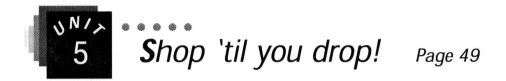

UNIT 5 — *Shop 'til you drop!* — Page 49

Presentation.

For general suggestions about how to use this page refer to the Introduction. Always ask the general questions about the illustration before moving on to the more specific questions suggested for each unit. (See specific questions for this unit below.)

For most beginning students:

Is this a house or a department store? *department store*

Is there one floor or two floors? *two floors*

Are there 5 or 6 people in the store? *6*

Is there 1 department or 4 departments in this store? *4*

Are the restrooms on the first or second floor? *Second floor*

For low beginning students:

Is this a department store? *Yes*

Are there 4 people? *No, there are 6 people.*

Is there only one department? *No, there are 4.*

Are the restrooms on this (Point.) floor? *Yes*

For more advanced students:

How many people are in the picture? *6*

Where are they? *in a department store*

What are the they doing? *Selling things, shopping, trying on clothes*

How many departments are there in this picture? *4*

Point to the customers. How many customers are there? *4*

Point to the salesclerks? How many salesclerks are there? *2*

Look, listen, and point./Listen and write.

Follow the Introduction. Then play the tape or use the tapescript. Have students complete page 49.

Follow-up activity.

Talk about department stores. Brainstorm a list of department stores in your local area. Find out at which stores your students shop. Make a list on the board with the names of these stores.

Optional follow-up.

The next day give students a tape dictation. See the Introduction for details.

More shopping.   Page 50

Write: *Men's Clothes, Women's Clothes, Children's Clothes,* and *Housewares* on the board.

Ask students to point to each department as you say the words. Ask students, "*What can you buy in the women's clothes department?*" Ask about each department. List these responses on the board under each department pictured: *Men's Clothes, Women's Clothes, Children's Clothes,* and *Housewares.*

Example:

Women's Clothes: dresses   Children's Clothes: children's socks

Men's Clothes: ties   Housewares: dishes

Follow the tape or read the tapescript.

Follow-up activity.

Bring in a brochure from a local department store that shows the layout of the store. See if students can find the departments on page 50. Underline them.

What color is the coat?   Page 51

Have students cover the bottom part of the page with a sheet of paper and look only at the clothing in the top section. Review the clothing items on the page. Make sure students can identify/name each one. Review color words.

Note: In some localities tennis shoes are known as sneakers.

Follow the tape for **Look, listen, and point.**

Have students point to each of the departments. Ask, "*What clothes are in the women's department?*" for example.

Make a list on the board.

Follow the tape for **Listen and write.**

Answers:		
1. green	4. gray	7. (yes) Children's
2. blue and white	5. orange	8. (yes) Women's
3. white and green	6. red	9. (yes) Men's

Assign workbook pages 33 and 34.

Answers:

Page 33

1. shorts	5. hat	9. sandals	13. underwear
2. cap	6. suit	10. t-shirt	14. pants
3. coat	7. dress	11. tennis shoes (sneakers)	15. sweater
4. purse	8. tie	12. shirt	16. socks

Answers:

Page 34

red, red dress, black, wearing, sandals; blue, blue dress, brown, wearing, shoes; blue, wearing, blue suit, black shoes, wearing black shoes.

Follow-up activities.

Play the game "*What am I wearing?*"

Choose one student and have the student stand in front of the room. Give students 1 minute to look at the student. Send the student out of the room and have the class brainstorm what the student was wearing. Have the student return. Check for accuracy. Do this two or three times.

Play the guessing game *"Who is it?"*

Have students look at someone in the room and write on an index card what he/she is wearing. Collect the index cards, read them aloud, and have the class identify the "wearer."

Small, medium, and large   Page 52

Follow the tape for **Listen and read.**

Then divide students into pairs and have them practice the dialog by using the clothes and sizes on the right. Model one or two conversations before assigning.

Follow-up activity.

Bring in various items of men's and women's clothing. Divide students into small groups. Give some clothing to each group and have them practice selling/buying it.

Can you tell me what you're wearing?   Page 53

Review clothing and colors by asking what students are wearing.

Model the conversation with a student. Show students how to start a tally (JHT II) for each item. Later, they can add up the tally marks to find the totals for each box on the chart.

Have students mingle and ask classmates the questions and make a tally for each item and color.

Let's go shopping.   Page 54

Allow students to "talk" to each other about the ads. Encourage students to respond to questions. Restate their ideas in acceptable English as you write your words on the board. Read aloud what you have written.

Put the word *ad* on the board and see if students know what it means. Show them the ads on the page and say, *"These are ads."* Bring in ads from your newspaper as samples. Write the word *price* on the board to see if they know what it means. Write the word *sale* on the board. See if they know what a sale is. Write *special* on the board. Explain that *special* and *sale* are similar. The price is less than the regular price.

Ask students to point to the word *Specials,* and the word *Sale.*

Ask students questions about each of the ads.

"How much are the pants?" "How much is the purse?" "Where are T-shirts on sale?" "How much are the dresses at Graces Shoppe?" "How much are the men's hats?" "Where can you buy shoes on sale?" etc.

Read aloud, *"You have $100. What do you want to buy?"* Tell students to make a list of things they want to buy with their $100. They should write the name of the item, how many they want to buy of each item, and the cost. Have them add to find the total cost.

Follow-up activity.

Divide students into pairs and have them practice describing what they would like to buy. Encourage the partners to ask questions such as those shown below.

"What item do you want to buy?"

"How many do you want to buy?"

"How much will it cost?"

Assign workbook pages 35 and 36.

Answers: Part A

    1. a pair of socks, a coat, and a pair of pants

    2. a suit and a pair of shorts

    3. a coat, a suit, and a pair of pants

    4. a sweater, a coat, a suit, a pair of pants

Answers: Part B

    a. Carmen is.   b. Carlos is.   c. Rose is.   d. Ali is.

Answers: Page 36

Rose		Carmen		Hiroshi	
Cash $20.00		Cash $15.00		Cash $120.00	
pants	$ 8.50	sweater	$11.90	sweater	$11.90
shorts	6.85	socks	.60	coat	25.00
TOTAL	15.35	TOTAL	12.50	suit	60.40
change:	4.65	change	2.50	pants	8.50
				TOTAL	105.80
				change	14.20

Assign workbook page 37 Part A.

Answers: Part A

    1. small   2. medium   3. large

Do the Jazz chant *The Price is Right* shown on workbook page 38.

Party! Party! Party   Page 55

See the Introduction for specific instructions.

Have students cover the **Listen and read** with a piece of paper.

Write the words *birthday party* on the board. Allow students to "talk" to each other about the picture. Encourage students to respond to questions. Restate their ideas in acceptable English and write them on the board. Read what you have written on the board.

Answer the questions. Follow the tape or read the tapescript.

Answers:
1. Carmen is having a party.   3. Celebrating Carmen's birthday
2. Many of her friends   4. November 13.

Follow-up activity.

Have students close their book. Do a focused listening. See the Introduction for instructions. If anyone is having a birthday soon, write the birthday song on the board and teach it to the class.

Cooperative learning line up.

Follow the instructions for line up in the Introduction.

Have students write their birthday on a file card.

Have them line up in order from January through December by their birthday.

Find your birthday.   Page 56

Review the months of the year. **Assign workbook page 37 Part B.**

 UNIT 5 *Crossword Puzzle* *Page 37* Part B: Complete the page as indicated.

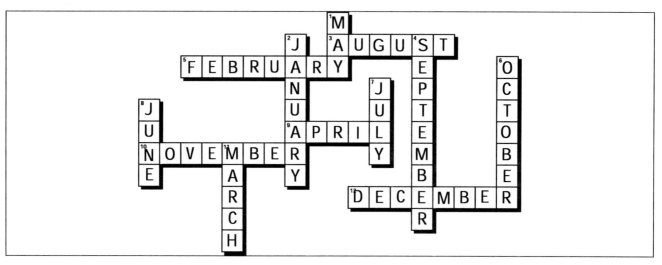

Assign workbook page 38 Parts A and B.

This page can be used to work on student-produced publications. As a model, draw a picture and then write a short paragraph about a birthday party you or one of your children had. Photocopy it and hand it out to the class. Ask them to use it to write a story about a birthday party in their family. If there is a computer available in the class or if there is a computer lab, have students word process their stories. Print these out and display them or develop a class book for each student of all finished stories. Ask students to bring in a photo of the party if possible. If a scanner is available, photos can be scanned and placed electronically with the students' stories. If no scanner is available, have students place the photos with their stories and then photocopy them.

I'm so happy!   Page 57

Write the words *happy, surprised, excited,* and *thrilled* on the board. Read aloud and have students practice pronouncing the words. Explain that the words can have the same meaning. Any of them can be said in answer to the question *"How you are feeling on your birthday?"*

Follow the tape or read the tapescript.

Divide students into pairs and have them practice the conversation with a partner.

Too small? Too large?   Page 58

Follow the tape for **Listen and read.**

Practice.

Point to each of the eight pictures and ask students what the problem is.

Answers:			
1. too large	3. too large	5. too small	7. too small
2. too small	4. too small	6. too large	8. too large

Have students practice the conversation in pairs.

Follow-up activity.

Bring some old clothes to class. Ask volunteers to try them on and talk about how they fit.

Review.   Page 59

Follow the tape or play the tapescript.

Answers: Listen and check answers.			
1. a	2. b	3. a	4. c

I can do this!

See the Introduction for instructions on ways to use this page.

Assign the Crossword Puzzle and Wordsearch, Workbook pages 39 and 40.

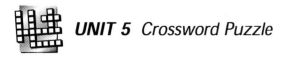 **UNIT 5** *Crossword Puzzle*

 UNIT 5 *Wordsearch*

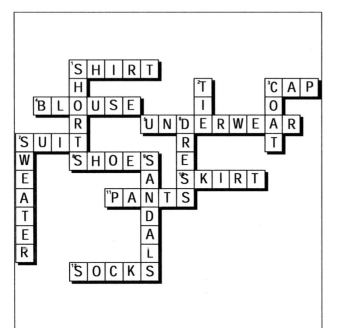

B	C	Y	B	D	L	O	H	L	B	U	V		I
D	L	C	T	I	E	U	R	L	O	X	U	M	K
R	S	A	V	V	P	N	C	V	V	K	M	N	T
E	A	P	T	X	U	D	O	P	O	C	V	Z	H
S	N	K	C	M	R	E	A	G	C	V			S
S	D	Q	D	P	S	R	T	A	P	P	Q	E	K	H
F	A	E	F	R	E	W	G	F	U	P	E	S	O
S	L		G	I	H	E	X	U	P	N	X	E	R
X		S	R	S	A	A	Q	N	X	E	A	H	T
H	O	K	E	I	T	R	P	C	Y	S	H	S
P	C	I	P	A	N	T	S	P	M	M	B	R
O	K	R	N	J	I	S	N	T	C	V	A	D
L	S	T	S	W	E	A	T	E	R	W	T	H	T
L	N	S	H	I	R	T	B	L	O	U	S	E	E

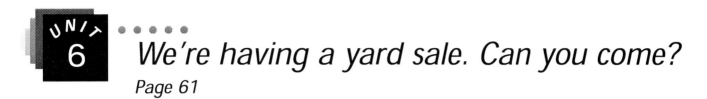

Presentation.

For general suggestions about how to use this page refer to the Introduction. Always ask the general questions about the illustration before moving on to the more specific questions suggested for each unit. (See specific questions for this unit below.)

Write the words *yard sale* on the board. Find out what the students know about yard sales by brainstorming with them and writing on the board what they say.

Make sure that students identify the answers to the following:

> When are yard sales usually held?
> Where are they held?
> How do people learn about them?

Follow the Introduction. Then follow the tape or read aloud the dialog between José and Van.

Answers:		
1. to a yard sale	2. tomorrow	3. nine o'clock

Practice.

Have students decide how Van Ly is going. Divide students into pairs and ask each pair to decide. Then discuss their conclusions as a whole class activity.

Follow-up activity.

Bring in the classified section of some newspapers. Have students find a yard/garage sale and read the ad to the class.

Optional follow-up activity.

The next day do a tape dictation. See the Introduction for details.

Assign workbook pages 41, 42, and 43.

Look at José's map.   Page 62

Review the vocabulary words on the page. Follow the tape or use the tapescript.

Follow-up activity.

Divide students into small groups and have them create a map of the local area surrounding the school. Encourage each group to share their maps with the whole class.

Answers:	
1. restaurant	4. drugstore
2. department store	5. Center Street and Main Street
3. parking garage	6. Center Street, shoe store, the plumber

How can I get from Duttonville School to the park?   Page 63

Review the vocabulary on the page.

Follow the tape or use the tapescript. Using the map on page 62, have student pairs practice giving directions in the Practice section. Model a few for the students.

Answers

1. Turn left on First Avenue. Walk to Main. Turn left on Main. Turn right on Grand and you will see the bank on the right side.
2. Turn left on Oak Street. Turn right on grand Avenue. You will see the market on the left side.
3. Walk straight on Oak Street to Orange. Turn right on Orange. You will see the theater on the left side.
4. Turn left on Grand Ave. Turn right on Main Street. Turn left on First Avenue. You will see the post office on the right side.
5. Turn left on Oak Street. Turn left on Third Ave. City Hall is on the corner of Third Avenue and Main Street.
6. Turn left on First Avenue. Turn right on Main. Walk to Second Avenue.

Assign workbook pages 44 and 45. Follow the jazz chant instructions for *"How can I get there?"*

Answers: Page 44

1. restaurant	4. drugstore	7. bakery
2. department store	5. Main and Center Street	
3. parking garage	6. Center Street between the shoe store and the plumber.	

Glad to see you!   page 64

Allow students to "talk" to each other about the picture. Encourage students to respond to questions. Restate their ideas in acceptable English and write them on the board. Read aloud what you have written.

Follow the tape or read the dialog aloud. Have students answer the questions in pairs.

Answers:

1. They are at a yard sale.
2. Looking at things on sale, and José is helping Grandpa to buy things.
3. Answers will vary.

Pots and Pans   Page 65

Follow the directions in the Introduction for vocabulary pages.

Assign workbook page 46.

Follow-up activity.

Have students categorize the items on the page. Use the categories on the Yard Sale sign and write additional categories, such as Kitchen Items and Furniture.

Optional follow-up activity.

Have students alphabetize the items on the page.

Review.   Page 66

Follow the tape or use the tapescript.

Answers:		
1. rug, N	4. sofa, D	7. table, L
2. lamp, G	5. chair, C	8. coat, F
3. blue dress, A	6. teakettle, Q	9. books, O

Assign workbook pages 47 and 48.

Ask your partner.   Pages 67 and 68; 69 and 70

Review all the vocabulary on both pages.

Review the question: *How do you spell that, please?*

Also review the question: *"What is number _____ ?"* for Page 67 and *"How much is the _____ ?"* for Pages 69 and 70.

Let's figure it out?   Page 71

Follow the directions for Information Gap activities in the Introduction.

Have student pairs read and practice the two dialogs at the top of the page. Then review the money amounts on the page. Monitor to make sure that students are saying the right amounts.

Note: Student B will be using plural forms of each noun.

Optional activity for more advanced students.

Have student A cover the B side. Student A should ask, *How many _____ are there? How much are the _____?*

Answers:					
1. $.15	2. $11.00	3. $4.50	4. $14.00	5. $.50	6. $10.50

Follow-up activity.

If it is possible, have a yard sale at your school or take a field trip to a local yard sale. If neither is possible, bring in items from your house for a make-believe yard sale. Have students price them and then simulate a yard sale.

I can do this!

See the Introduction for instructions on ways to use this page.

Assign the Crossword Puzzle and Wordsearch, Workbook pages 47 and 48.

UNIT 6 Crossword Puzzle

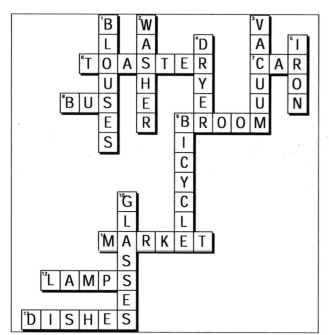

UNIT 6 Wordsearch

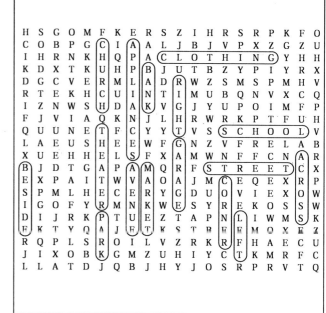

Presentation.

For general suggestions about how to use this page refer to the Introduction. Always ask the general questions about the illustration before moving on to the more specific questions suggested for each unit. (See specific questions for this unit below.)

For most beginning students:

Are they standing in the street or in a department store? *in the street*

Is it raining or sunny? *raining*

Are there 7 or 8 people? *8*

Is there a man or a woman in front of the car? *man*

For low beginning students:

Is this a street corner? *yes*

Are there 7 people? *No, there are 8 people.*

Is it raining? *yes*

Is a man hit by a car? *yes*

For more advanced students:

How many people are in the picture? *8*

Where are they? *on a street corner*

What are the they doing? *standing*

What is happening in this picture? *A man is hit by a car.*

Follow the Introduction. Then play the tape or use the tapescript. Have students complete the page. Then discuss their answers as a group.

Follow-up activities.

1. *Focused Listening:* See the Introduction for details.

2. *Tape Dictation:* The next day do a tape dictation. See the Introduction for details.

Who? What?   Page 74

Show students how to use the pictures to ask questions that begin with *Who* or *What.*

Examples: Who is standing?   What is Van Ly holding?

Brainstorm with the class as many questions as possible and write them on the board.

Follow the tape or read the questions.

Answers:		
1. José and Van	4. 911.	7. some people
2. a man	5. the traffic accident	8. a trash can
3. He is hit by a car.	6. an umbrella	

Optional presentation for more advanced students.

Divide students into pairs. Have them first write the answers. Next have one member of each pair ask the questions and the partner answers the questions with his/her book closed. Exchange roles.

Call 911.   Page 75

Write the word *emergency* on the board. Discuss what an emergency is. Next talk about 911 emergencies. Ask students, *"What information is required for 911 calls?"* (type of emergency, exact location with cross streets.)

Help students understand what cross streets are by indicating the cross streets of your school and the exact location of the school.

Listen and answer.

Follow the tape or read the conversation, then ask each question.

> *Answers:*
>   1. 911   2. This is an emergency.   3. place/where   4. Main Street and Grand Ave.

Ask students to draw a map of the area around their home and to include cross streets.

Follow-up activity.

Divide students into small groups. If possible, give a tape recorder to each group. Show them how to use the tape recorder to record and play back. While two students practice calling 911 the other students record the conversation. Continue until each person has a conversation on tape. Collect the tapes and use for assessment.

What's the emergency?   Page 76

Follow the tape or read the tapescript for both sections of the page.

> *Answers:*
>   a. 2   b. 6   c. 1   d. 5   e. 3   f. 4

Assign workbook page 49.

> *Workbook answers:* page 49
>   1. bleeding   2. robbery   3. fire   4. drowning   5. traffic accident   6. choking

Ask your partner.   Page 77

Read the conversation aloud with the students. Have pairs practice the 6 conversations.

How's the weather today?   Page 78

Write the question, *"How's the weather today?"* on the board.

Then write the 8 weather words on the board.

Follow the tape or use the tapescript.

Have student's fill in the **Write** activity.

Follow-up activity.

Write the following on the board and have students complete each statement.

Today the weather is _____.

Yesterday the weather was _____.

Tomorrow I think it will _____.

Have students read what they wrote. Make a class prediction about tomorrow's weather.

Assign workbook page 50.

Answers:

   a. cold   b. hot   c. raining   d. snowing   e. windy   f. sunny   g. foggy   h. cloudy

Ask your partner.　Page 79

Review the pictures on the page. Pair students and have them practice asking questions.

Have them practice four times. The first time one person asks *Yes/No* questions and the other answers. Then they change places. The third time one person asks, *"How is the weather today?"* and the partner answers. Then they change places.

Assign workbook page 51.

Carlos goes to the emergency room.　Page 80

Review the items in the picture on page 80 by having students point to the following: *the ambulance, emergency room entrance, flashing lights,* and *the stop sign.*

Ask the students, *"Does the ambulance need to stop at the stop sign?"*

Talk about rules of the road in regard to an ambulance.

Ask, *"What do you do if you are driving and you see an ambulance with its siren on and lights flashing?"*

Follow the tape or read the paragraph aloud, then ask the questions.

Answers:

   1. the paramedics   2. an ambulance   3. the doctor and nurse   4. medical form

Listen and Read.　Page 81

Talk about the picture with the students and write what they say on the board. Try to get as much discussion about what is happening in this picture as possible.

Follow the tape or use the tapescript.

Follow-up activity.

Have students write a class story. See the Language Experience technique in the Introduction. Tell them to use the words on page 81.

Assign workbook page 52.

Answers:

a. ambulance	c. hospital	e. emergency room	g. nurses
b. paramedics	d. patient	f. doctors	h. medical form

What's the matter with Carlos?   Page 82

Follow the tape or use the tapescript. Have students practice the conversation in pairs substituting various parts of the body in place of the word *leg*.

Follow-up activity.

Simon Says: Have the whole class stand up. The objective of this game is to remain standing. Say, *"Simon says point to your _____."* (Name a body part.) If you say *Simon says*, the students point. If you say, *"Point to your_____."* with no preface of *Simon says*, the students should not point. If anyone points, he/she must sit down. The objective is to be the last person standing.

Review.   Page 83

Match the pictures.

> *Answers:*
>
> 1. e   2. c   3. g   4. a   5. f   6. d   7. h   8. b
>
> *Fill in the blanks answers from top to bottom:*
>
> head, neck, chest, arm, hand, leg, foot, and back

Assign workbook pages 53 and 54.

> *Answers:* Page 53
>
> a. neck   b. arm   c. chest   d. foot   e. back   f. hand   g. head   h. leg

Do the jazz chant *Body Parts* by following the directions in the Introduction.

> *Answers:* Page 54
>
> 4   2   1   5   3
>
> *Order of sentences:*
>
> Carlos is crossing the street.
>
> A car hits Carlos.
>
> José calls 911.
>
> The ambulance takes Carlos to the emergency room.
>
> The doctors and nurses examine Carlos.

I can do this!

See the Introduction page for instructions on ways to use this page.

Assign the Crossword Puzzle and Wordsearch, Workbook pages 55 and 56.

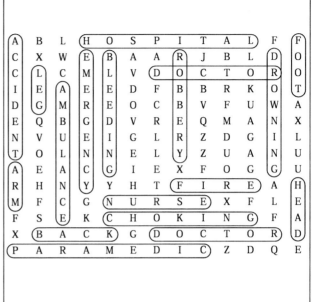

Somebody is sick with a cold. *Page 85*

Presentation.

For general suggestions about how to use this page refer to the Introduction. Always ask the general questions about the illustration before moving on to the more specific questions suggested for each unit. (See specific questions for this unit below.)

For most beginning students:

Is Carlos sick or healthy? *sick*

Is Carlos in the bedroom or the living room? *in the living room*

Is Carlos lying on the bed or on the couch? *on the couch*

Point to the bedroom.

For low beginning students:

Is Carlos sick? *Yes.*

Is Carlos in the bedroom? *No.*

Is Carlos lying on the couch? *Yes.*

For more advanced students:

Where is Carlos? *in the living room on the couch*

How does he feel? *sick*

What is he doing? *resting*

Listen and read.

Have students practice the dialog. Review different kinds of illness by brainstorming with students. Write the different kinds of illness on the board. (*sore throat, cold, fever, cough,* etc.)

Using the focused listening technique, have students listen to the dialog again and answer the question: *What's the matter with Carlos?*

Next have students listen as you read each question aloud. Pause after each question and elicit the answer. Have students open their books and write the answers to the questions.

Follow-up activity.

Have students ask and answer questions in pairs.

Divide students into small groups. Have each group write one additional question that isn't asked.

Collect the questions from each group and dictate them. Have students write both the questions and the answers.

Check the answers by having students write them on the board.

Assign page 57 of the workbook. Each Health Information Form will vary.

What's the matter?   Page 86

Follow the tape or use the tapescript.

Follow-up activity.

Discuss when to use *sore* and when to use *hurts*.

Make two columns on the board. Write:

I have a sore _____.   My _____ hurts.

Divide students into small groups. Have them write sentences using various parts of the body with either the word *sore* or *hurts*.

For example: I have a sore throat.   My knee hurts.

Have groups write their sentences on the board.

Assign workbook pages 58 and 59.

Answers:

What's the matter? Page 58

    1. Ali has a fever.   3. Carmen has a cold.   5. Hiroshi has a cough.

    2. Carlos is sick.   4. Petra has a sore throat.

What hurts? Page 59

    1. Van's back hurts.   3. Charlie's stomach hurts.   5. Pedro's tooth hurts.

    2. Makeba's ear hurts.   4. Bic's knee hurts.   6. Rose's head hurts.

Listen.   Page 87

Follow the tape or use the tapescript.

Answers:

1. yes	3. no	5. yes	7. yes	9. no	11. yes
2. no	4. yes	6. yes	8. no	10. yes	12. yes

Small Group Practice.

Divide students into small groups of 5 or 6. Have them practice by asking questions about each person.

Follow-up activity.

Make a copy of page 87 for each student. Have students cut the pictures apart. Direct students to make a paper grid by folding their paper down to form equal halves, then across to form 3 parts; six boxes in all when opened up. Their paper will look like this:

1.	2.	3.
4.	5.	6.

Have students number each square on their paper, 1-6. Model the activity by drawing a grid on the board. Number each box on the board.

- Say, *"Number 1, Charlie has a stomachache."* (*"Charlie's stomach hurts."*)
- Tape picture 12 in the first box on the board.
- Have students place Charlie's picture in box 1.
- Do this until all the boxes are filled.
- Repeat the activity by placing different pictures in the boxes.
- Model the following pair activity with a student.
    1. Sit face to face.
    2. Use a file folder to act as a barrier.
    3. Tell the student where to put the pictures.
    4. Check your papers.

After you finish placing 6 pictures in the boxes, exchange roles with the student. Divide the students into pairs and have them practice the activity the same way.

Review.   Page 88

Presentation.

Listen and read along with the tape.

Review the vocabulary at the bottom of the page. Make a transparency of the conversation or copy the conversation on the board. Model how students can practice the conversation by substituting words on the board. Divide students into pairs and have them practice the conversation a few times. Walk around the room and monitor as students practice.

Follow-up activity.

Use the disappearing conversation technique described in the Introduction.

Optional follow-up activity.   *(This activity requires 3-5 tape recorders.)*

Divide the students into small groups. Give each group a tape recorder and a blank tape. Model how to operate the tape recorder. Instruct each group to tape each pair in their group as they practice the dialog. Collect completed tapes to review them at home. Follow-up by offering constructive suggestions to the students.

Ask your partner.   Pages 89 and 90

Follow the general directions described in the Introduction.

Answers for Student A:	*Answers for Student B:*
Rose's head hurts.	Ali has a fever.
Pedro's tooth hurts.	Makeba's ear hurts.
Hiroshi has a cough.	Petra has a sore throat.

Feeling better?   Page 91

Play the tape or use the tapescript.

Assign workbook page 60.

Before having students complete this page of the workbook, be sure to review the vocabulary.

Answers: Page 60

top shelf:
aspirin, cough syrup, nose drops

middle shelf:
pills (in the middle)

bottom shelf:
ear drops, (nothing), cold medicine

table:
bowl of chicken soup (left), cup of hot tea (right).

What's the matter today?   Page 92

Presentation.

Make an overhead transparency of the page or write the conversation on the board. Read aloud and have students read after you. Model how to correct the illness by using a remedy. Divide students into pairs and have them practice all five conversations. Monitor students as they practice.

Follow-up activity.

Pair Dictation: Using one of the five dialogs that the pairs created, follow the directions in the Introduction. Have pairs do a pair dictation.

Carlos, Juan, and Pedro share an apartment.   Page 93

Preparation.

Using the opener procedure detailed in the Introduction, elicit information about the picture.

Find out the information: *What games do they play?*

Presentation.

Follow the tape or use the tapescript.

Answers:

1. apartment	3. daughters	5. work	7. call	9. Saturdays
2. sons	4. healthy	6. save	8. play	10. Sundays

Follow-up activity.

Dictation: Use the directions detailed in the Introduction.

How do Juan, Carlos, and Pedro stay healthy?   Page 94

Preparation.

Write these words on the board: *every day   on Saturday and Sunday   daily   every night*

Make sure that students know that *daily* means the same as *every day*.

Practice the pronunciation of *daily*.

Write a few sentences about yourself using the above vocabulary.

Presentation.

Make a transparency of the page or copy the 6 sentences on the board. Follow the tape or use the tapescript.

Have each student write the answer to the question at the bottom of the page: What do you do to try to stay healthy? Encourage them to share their answers with the group.

Follow-up activity.

As students are writing the answer to the question, walk around the room and note what the students do. Try to find 3 answers that are the most common. Write the three most common activities on index cards and place each one in a corner of the room. In the fourth corner, write *other* on an index card. Have students stand up and divide into one of the four corners.

Expansion.

Using the numbers of students in each corner, have groups make bar graphs.

Assign workbook pages 61 and 62. Use the jazz chant *Staying Healthy*.

Answers:	
1. I shower everyday.	Carlos showers everyday.
2. I rest on Saturdays and Sundays.	Pedro rests on Saturday and Sundays
3. I exercise daily.	Carlos exercises daily.
4. I eat fruits and vegetables everyday.	Carlos eats fruits and vegetables everyday.
5. I sleep eight hours every night.	Carlos sleeps eight hours every night.
6. I brush my teeth every day.	Carlos brushes his teeth every day.

Follow-up activity.

Develop a student produced publication. See the Introduction for daily habits.

Review.   Page 95

Preparation.

Review the vocabulary on the chart.

Presentation.

Make a transparency of the page or copy the chart on the board. Divide students into pairs or in small groups. Direct them to use the information on page 86 and 94 to complete the chart. Check off several answers as examples. Then have groups check off the answers on the board.

Carmen				√						
Petra							√			√
Ali	√									
Juan								√		√
Hiroshi									√	
Pedro			√			√				
Carlos		√			√					√

Follow-up activity.

Question Grid: Follow instructions in the Introduction using 2 columns and 6 rows.

Question:

What do you do daily to stay healthy?

I can do this!   Page 96

Follow the general directions in the Introduction.

Assign the Crossword Puzzle and Wordsearch, Workbook pages 63 and 64.

 UNIT 8 *Crossword Puzzle*

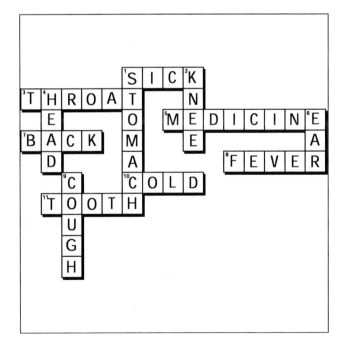

 UNIT 8 *Wordsearch*

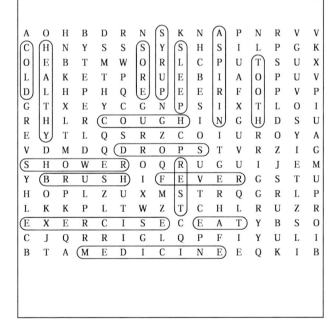

Grandpa wants to take the bus. *Page 97*

Presentation.

For general suggestions about how to use this page refer to the Introduction. Always ask the general questions about the illustration before moving on to the more specific questions suggested for each unit. (See specific questions for this unit below.)

For most beginning students:

Is Grandpa at the bus stop or at home? *at the bus stop*

Point to the bus stop sign.

Is Rose waving or eating? *waving*

Point to the bus.

For low beginning students:

Is Grandpa at home? *No.*

Is there a bus waiting? *Yes.*

Is Grandpa waving? *No.*

Is Grandpa pointing at the bus? *Yes.*

For more advanced students:

Where are Grandpa, Rose, and May? *They are at the bus stop.*

What are Grandpa and Rose doing? *They are seeing May off to school on a bus.*

Where is May going? *to school*

Have students close their books and practice the dialog by following the tape.

Using the focused listening technique, have students listen to the dialog again and answer this question: What does Grandpa want? *He wants to take the city bus to his school.*

Listen and Circle.

Follow the tape or use the tapescript. Discuss the meaning of *Transit Authority* and *Good for one month.*

Follow-up activity.

Put signs up in the four corners of the classroom that read *bus, car, walk, other.*

Have students go into the corner based on how they get to school.

Then ask students to graph the results.

Find out how many of the students who take the bus have a bus pass.

Discuss each bus pass. Ask: *How long is it good for? Where did you buy it? When did you buy it?*

Read the signs on the way to school.   Page 98

Presentation.

Ask the students what they see pictured on page 98. Elicit *street signs*.

Ask them, *"Do you know what each sign means?"*

Listen and read.

Play the tape and have students listen.

Follow-up activity.

Materials required: Index cards, glue, and scissors

Photocopy the page, if possible, and have students cut apart each sign and each sentence.

Give each student 9 index cards. Have them cut each card in half.

Have them glue the picture on one half of the card, and the written description on the other half.

These cards can be used in three ways:

1. Play concentration.
   Divide students into pairs.
   Have one pair put their cards away.
   Have students mix the remaining set and place each card face down.
   Each student turns over two cards at a time. If the student gets a match, he/she gets the set.
   The person with the most sets is the "winner."

2. Mingle Activity
   Borrow enough sets to cover the class. For example, if you have 30 students, use four sets, if you have 15 students use two sets.
   Have students put away the other sets of cards.
   Deal out the cards, one to each student. Have students find their partners. If you have an odd number of students, tell the class that one student will have no partner.

3. Play "Go Fish."
   Divide students into groups of three or four.
   Use two sets of cards for each group.
   Mix and deal out four cards to each student.
   Students ask for cards they want to secure to make a match.
   Examples: "Do you have *Do not enter*?" or "Do you have *Don't go there!*"
   If a student has the corresponding card, that student should give it to the player who asked for it. If they don't have it, then they say, "Go Fish." and the student picks from the pile.
   Every matched set is put down in front of the student who made the match.
   The student with the most pairs is the winner.

Assign workbook page 65.

This is a matching activity. Have students read Part A and then write the corresponding sentence under each sign.

Find the signs.   Page 99

Presentation.

Review the directions in Unit 6.

Make sure that students understand the meaning of *on the corner of, on the (store), on (street name).*

If possible, make an overhead transparency of the page or enlarge the page so that everyone can see the details on the map. Practice pronouncing the street names with the students. Say a street name and have them point to it as they say it. Point to each letter and ask, *"What is this letter?"*

Once students are thoroughly familiar with the map, divide them into pairs and have them find the 7 signs.

Answers:

    1. g   2. b   3. d   4.a   5. h   6. c   7. e

Follow-up activity.

As a group, have the class draw a map of the school neighborhood. Then ask them to put in signs where they appear in actuality.

How do you come to school?   Page 100

Follow the tape or use the tapescript. **Note:** for *on foot* you can introduce the sentences *"I walk to school."* or *"He/She walks to school."*

Assign workbook page 66.

Answers:

    1. c   2. d   3. g.   4. f   5. b.   6. a   7. e

Ask your classmates.   Page 101

Presentation.

Write the question *"How do you come to school?"* on the board. Ask a few students. Make a transparency or copy the chart from Page 101 on the board. Say, *"Van comes to school by bus. How does Carlos come to school?"* Elicit the answer *"by bicycle"* (See page 100.) and put an X under bicycle.

Practice.

Have students ask ten different people in the room, *"How do you come to school?"* They should ask each interviewee his/her name and put an X under the correct column. Remind students that they can ask, *"How do you spell your name?"*

Follow-up activity.

As a group, make a class chart. Indicate how each student in the class comes to school.

Complete the bar graph.

This is best done as a whole class activity.

Using the class chart, show students how to total the number of students using each different mode of transportation. Have them put the number on the line indicated in the chart. Have students complete the bar graph. Show students how to darken with a pencil or color in squares for the different numbers. If crayons are available, students can use different colors for each of the 7 entries on the graph.

Assign workbook pages 67 and 68. Answers will vary.

Grandpa's ride home on the bus.   Page 102

Elicit information about the picture. Ask students, *"What do you see in the picture?"* If students need encouragement, say, *"stores?, street?, avenue?, What's this?"* (Point to the bus.)

Follow the tape or use the tapescript.

Answers:		
1. drugstore	3. gas station	5. movie theater
2. laundromat	4. restaurant	6. bakery

Ask your partner.   Pages 103-104

Presentation.

Review the places on the map on page 102. Write the sentences from Page 103 on the board. Have students practice reading them. Follow the directions in the Introduction for Information Gap activities.

Pair students and assign one person in each pair as either student "A" or student "B." Have the "A" students open their books to Page 103 and the "B" students turn to Page 104. Have students complete the activity and then check for accuracy. Walk around the room to help students as needed to complete the activity.

Assign workbook page 69.

Answers:											
1. f	2. c	3. h	4. g	5. b	6. k	7. i	8. e	9. d	10. l	11. j	12. a

Can you find the address?   Page 105

If possible, make a transparency of the page. (Note: This is the same map that appears on page 99, but 4 addresses have been added.) Review the map. Call attention to the addresses shown on the map. Go over the places and the street names. Pair students and have them work together to find the location of each building. Check the students' written work with the whole class.

Follow-up activity.

Pair students. Have them look only at the map. (They should use a piece of paper to cover the text.) Have them ask each other where various buildings are.

Can you read the bus schedule?   Page 106

Make a transparency of the page or copy the bus schedule on the board. Show students how to read the schedule for each bus from left to right. You may wish to dramatize the stops of the first bus by assigning four students street stops (Orange Avenue, Grand Avenue, Main Street, and Grace Street). Play the part of the conductor, call out each stop, and have the student who lives there "get off the bus."

Review the bus schedule with the class.

Follow the tape or read aloud 1 through 5 and ask students to fill in the answers.

Answers:

1. 8:20 AM   2. 10:00 PM   3. four times on the hour   4. three times on the hour

5. 2:30, 2:40; 4:20, 6:30; 8:20, 8:40; 10:30, 10:40

Follow-up activity.

Bring in a bus/train schedule for your local area. Have students ask and answer questions about the local bus schedule.

Use workbook page 70.

Do the 2 jazz chants on page 70.

What time does your bus leave?   Page 107

Make a transparency of the page or write the bus schedules for the two busses on the board.

Ask students questions about each one. Use questions similar to, but not the same as the questions in the following reading activity.

Have students open their books to Page 107 and complete the activity.

Answers:

1. 2:30   2. #10 at 3:15, 3:30 PM   3. 4:00 PM   4. #10 at 3:15   5. 4:00 PM

I can do this!   Page 108

Follow the general directions in the Introduction.

Assign the Crossword Puzzle and Wordsearch, Workbook pages 71 and 72.

UNIT 9 *Crossword Puzzle*

 UNIT 9 *Wordsearch*

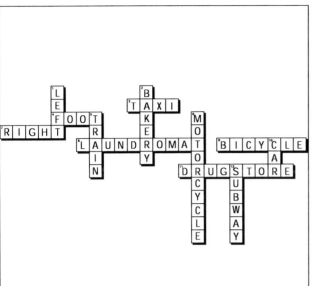

```
J  O  X  Q  R  E  S  T  A  U  R  A  N  T  J  D  E
X  Z  A  G  D  Y  Z  B  R  K  C  S  V  G  H  U  E
O  H  W  A  S  F  Z  U  V  G  Y  C  E  X  U  S  J
C  G  I  G  A  L  X  S  B  Y  S  H  H  L  D  C  F
Q  S  T  A  T  I  O  N  J  M  X  E  I  B  T  I  M
F  Q  V  T  W  W  L  B  I  Y  Q  D  C  P  A  J  B
V  E  M  F  A  P  R  N  P  X  V  U  L  I  X  P  A
D  I  P  M  Q  M  S  D  E  A  J  L  E  H  I  O  K
P  L  A  U  N  D  R  O  M  A  T  E  C  G  T  L  E
G  X  H  V  C  T  U  L  N  U  T  L  T  V  A  I  R
W  H  T  K  G  Q  E  I  F  E  H  W  P  G  N  C  Y
S  Z  L  S  Y  G  K  B  D  H  E  C  P  L  E  E  Q
B  P  O  V  R  E  O  R  E  M  A  E  O  R  I  L  F
O  X  P  N  H  O  C  A  J  B  T  X  M  A  H  S  R
X  I  K  K  V  T  Z  R  T  Q  E  I  Y  I  S  M  J
T  F  H  S  M  V  C  Y  U  E  R  T  H  N  L  C  Z
Y  F  I  R  E  D  E  P  A  R  T  M  E  N  T  J  B
```

53
• • • •

Presentation.

For general suggestions about how to use this page refer to the Introduction. Always ask the general questions about the illustration before moving on to the more specific questions suggested for each unit. (See specific questions for this unit below.)

For most beginning students:

Are they inside or outside the school? *outside*
Are they leaving or coming to school? *leaving*
Are they happy or sad? *happy*

For low beginning students:

Are they inside school? *No, they are outside.*
Are they leaving school? *Yes.*
Are they happy? *Yes.*

For more advanced students:

Where are they? *They are outside their school.*

What are they doing? *They are leaving school.*

How do they feel? *happy*

Write the words *full-time* (used here as an adjective) and *part time* (used as a noun) on the board. Make sure students understand these words. You may wish to write the following sentences on the board to clarify the difference in usage of these words.

I work full time at a department store.
I have a full-time job there.
I go to school part time.
I also have a part-time job at a supermarket.

With their books closed, have students practice the dialog by using the tape or tapescript.

Use the focused-listening technique. Then have students listen to the dialog again and answer the question: *How many jobs does Dominique have?*

Read and answer the questions.

Answers:	
1. Petra does.	4. The bank is.
2. Dominique does.	5. The factory is.
3. One is at a bank. The other is at a factory.	

Follow-up activity.

Ask all the students who work to stand up. Have students who are seated ask those standing, *"Do you work full time or do you have a part-time job?"* Help students make a chart by using the following information.

Total number of students = ____

Number of students who have part-time jobs ____

Number of students who work full time ____

What job do you want? Page 110

Presentation.

Make a transparency or copy the job notices on the board. Review each of the jobs with the class by having students first look at a picture, one at a time. Then ask, for example, *"What does a cook do?"* and point to the first picture. Elicit that a cook cooks food. Do this for each occupation. Then read each ad along with the class.

Next ask questions similar to, but not the same as, the writing activity.

Possible questions:

1. What does the bank need?
2. Does Spring Valley Library want a part-time custodian?
3. What does Tip Top Nails need?

Then pair students and have them write the answers. Check the work of each pair.

Follow-up activity.

Divide students into small groups. Have each group write an ad similar to the ones on page 110. Put all the ads together and have the groups write questions about the ads. Have groups exchange questions with another group and write the answers.

Assign workbook page 73.

Job	Hours	Salary	Full-time Job?	
			Yes	**No**
bank teller	M-F 9am-1pm	$ 8.00 an hour		X
cook	Sat. & Sun. 9-6	$ 8.00 an hour		X
custodian	M-W-F 6-12pm	$ 4.75 an hour		X
factory worker	M-F 8am-5pm	$ 6.75 an hour	X	
manicurist	M-F 8am-6pm	$ 5.25 an hour	X	
mechanic	M & W 8-5	$ 9.75 an hour		X
nurse	1am-8am	$ 18.75 an hour	X	
secretary	M-F 9am-5pm	$ 6.75 an hour	X	

Jobs, jobs, jobs.   Page 111

Presentation.

Review the 12 jobs in the shaded boxes at the top of the page. Then have students name each job. Play the tape or read the tapescript.

Answers:			
1. factory worker	4. food server	7. barber	10. nurse
2. teacher	5. construction worker	8. secretary	11. gardener
3. security guard	6. custodian	9. computer entry person	12. manicurist

Follow-up activity.

Materials required: Index cards, glue, and scissors

Photocopy the page and have students cut apart each of the 12 cards. Give each student 12 index cards. Tell students to cut each card in half. Have them glue the picture on one half of the card and the job title on the other half.

These cards can be used in three ways:

1. Play "Concentration."
   Divide students into pairs. Have one pair put their cards away.
   Have students mix the remaining set and place each card face down.
   Tell students to turn over two cards at a time. If they get a match, they get the set. The person with the most sets is the "winner."

2. Mingle activity
   Borrow enough sets to cover the class. For example, if you have 30 students, use five sets, if you have 18 students use three sets.
   Have students put away the other sets of cards.
   Deal out the cards, one to each student.
   Have students find their partner. (If there is an odd number of students, you can act as a partner.)

3. Play "Go Fish."
   Divide students into groups of three or four.
   Use two sets of cards for each group.
   Mix and deal four cards to each student.
   Tell students to take turns asking for a match card. Example: *"Do you have a card with a picture of a barber?"*
   If the student who is addressed has the matching card, that student must give it to the other player. If he/she doesn't have it, he/she should say, *"Go fish."* Students should put each match set in front of them. The student with the most matched sets is the winner.

What Do You Do?   Page 112

Dramatize the conversations at the top of the page. First assume the role of the woman asking the question. Then walk to your left and assume the role of the security guard. Also change your voice to match the way each character might talk. Invite volunteers to perform the same dialog exchange for the class.

Tell students to practice each of the 9 dialogs with a partner. The student who is asked the question should assume the identity of the character whose name appears at the bottom of the box. (Example: 1. Makeba) You might suggest that the student who assumes the identity perform a simple action related to his/her job. For example, "Makeba" could be filing or adding nail polish to imaginary hands. Then tell students to reverse roles and repeat the procedure in mixed order. Walk around the classroom and give help as needed.

Invite volunteers to perform one of the skits for the class.

Assign workbook pages 74 and 75.

Call attention to the dialog boxes at the top of page 74. Read the first question. Then point out the two ways that the question can be answered. (The second sentence reinforces the answer more explicitly: She is a TEACHER.) Repeat the procedure with the other box.

Then identify Pedro by pointing to him. Ask, *"Is Pedro a mechanic?"* Encourage the class to answer aloud by reading the two sentences given. Then ask the class to complete the two pages. Walk around the room and give help as necessary.

Hire or fire?   Page 113

Presentation.

Write the words *late, on time,* and *absent* on the board.

Then write on the board the time that your class begins.

Ask, *"What time is <u>on time</u>?"* Students should indicate the class starting time.

Then ask, *"What time is <u>late</u>?"* Students should indicate a time later than the starting class time.

Also ask, *"Who is <u>absent</u> today?"* Students should name any absent students.

Write the words *hire, fire,* and *lay off* on the board. Try to elicit meanings from students. If they have no clue, write: *fire = no job.* Then list possible reasons people are fired, such as: *absent a lot, comes to work late.* Then write the following: *hire = get job   lay off=no job because of no work.* (slow time)

Write *vacation* on the board and elicit its meaning.

Have students follow along with the tape or tapescript.

Read aloud with students.

She's on vacation.   Page 114

Discuss each picture and the caption under it. Make sure students understand the meaning of each caption. Encourage students to express as many ideas as possible about each picture by asking, *"Where is he/she? What is he/she doing?"*

Follow the tape or read each statement and tell students to circle the correct answer.

Listen and circle answers:			
1. a. on vacation	3. b. late	5. b. absent	7. a. a lay-off
2. a. hired	4. b. on time	6. a. fired	8. b. overtime

What do they do?　Page 115

Make a transparency of the page or write the 9 job titles on the board.

Point to a picture and have students name the job title. Then have students complete each sentence by writing the job titles on the lines provided.

Answers:

1. mechanic	4. cook	7. house painter
2. gardener	5. truck driver	8. seamstress
3. secretary	6. bank teller	9. barber

Notes: 1. Instead of *barber*, students may use *haircutter* or *hair stylist*.

2. You may wish to point out that the word *seamstress* is usually used for a female and the word *tailor* is used for a male.

Assign workbook pages 76 and 77.

Interview your classmates.　Page 116

Ask students to mingle in the classroom and ask 10 classmates, "*____, what do you do?*" The student asking the question should write each name and occupation on the chart at the top of the page.

As a group, discuss the bottom chart "My Dream Job." Encourage students to suggest the type of job they would most like to have and tell why. After sufficient time has passed in discussion, have students complete the information on their individual charts.

Assign workbook page 78.

Ask your partner.　Pages 117 and 118

Presentation.

Review the occupations. Write the occupations on the board. Have students practice reading them. Follow the directions in the Introduction for Information Gap activities.

Pair students and assign one person in each pair as either "A" or "B". Have the "A" students open to page 117 and the "B" students open to page 118. Have students complete the activity and then check for accuracy. Walk around the room and offer help to students as needed to complete the activity.

Answers:

1. Ali fixes cars. He is a mechanic.
2. Pedro cuts grass. He is a gardener.
3. Rose types and answers the phone. She is a secretary.
4. Carlos builds houses. He is a construction worker.
5. Karim drives a truck. He is a truck driver.
6. Farima's sister helps sick people. She is a nurse.
7. Hiroshi's father paints houses. He is a house painter.
8. Petra's mother sews clothes. She is a seamstress.
9. Javier cuts hair. He is a barber.

Carmen applies for a job.   Page 119

If possible, make a transparency of the page or copy Carmen's application on the board. Review the application to make sure students understand all the words shown. Have students fill in the application using their own information. Help students as needed.

Follow-up activity.

Photocopy page 119. Pair students and have them interview a partner and fill in the form.

Workbook follow-up.

Follow the instructions in the Introduction for student produced publications.

I can do this!   Page 120

Follow the general directions in the Introduction.

Assign the Crossword Puzzle and Wordsearch, Workbook pages 79 and 80.

 UNIT 10 Crossword Puzzle

 UNIT 10 Wordsearch

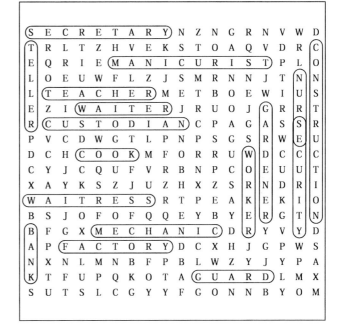

Dad works so hard. *Page 121*

Presentation.

For general suggestions about how to use this page refer to the Introduction. Always ask the general questions about the illustration before moving on to the more specific questions suggested for each unit. (See specific questions for this unit below.)

For most beginning students:

Point to the illustration of the Duval family who are eating dinner.

Use a transparency, if available; if not, use the text.

Ask, "Are they in a house or a school?" *house*

For low beginning students:

Are they in a house? *Yes*
Are they eating or singing? *eating*
Are they happy or sad? *happy*

For more advanced students:

Where are they? *at home in the dining room*
What are they doing? *They are eating dinner.*
How do they feel? *happy*
What is their relationship? *They are a family.*
Do you talk during your meals? If so, what do you talk about? (*Answers will vary.*)

Have students close their books and practice the dialog by following the tape or have students listen and read after you.

Using the focused listening technique (See the Introduction.), have students listen to the dialog again and answer the question: *What are they talking about?*

Pair students and have them answer the questions at the bottom of the student page.

> *Answers:*
>   1. eating dinner   2. Dominique   3. Jack is.   4. to Jack's office
>   5. Answers will vary. Have a discussion about what different students eat for dinner and then have students decide what they think the Duval family is eating.

Jack's office.   Page 122

Review the vocabulary words with the class. Follow the tape or tapescript.

At the office.   Page 123

Review the vocabulary words with the class.

Using an overhead projector or the text, have students point to each object as you name it.

Next divide students into pairs and have them practice pointing to the picture as their partner says a word.

With the same partners, have one student point and ask the partner, *"Is this a _____?"* The partner should answer, *"Yes, it is."* or *"No, it isn't."*

With the same partners, have students then practice asking, *"What is this?"* Again, the partner should answer.

For an advanced practice, have students ask, *"Where is the ____?"* Students can either point and answer, *"Here it is."* or respond using the prepositions from a previous chapter such as "the computer is next to the pencils and writing paper."

Follow-up activity.

Label the classroom. Give students index cards and have them label all the items in the classroom. Help students write the words including any words for things not in the office that you have in the classroom. Next have a discussion about which items are missing from the classroom that are in the office. Talk about why. Find out what items the students have at their workplace or home. List them on the board.

Assign workbook page 81.

Workbook answers:		
a. fax machine	d. telephone answering machine	g. typewriter
b. copier	e. file cabinet	h. calculator
c. computer keyboard	f. clothes-pressing machine	i. wastebasket

Review.   Page 124

Follow the tape or read the tapescript in the back of the book. Have students write the answers in the space provided.

Answers:							
1. H	2. D	3. A	4. F	5. B	6. G	7. C	8. E

Follow-up activity.

Pair students and assign one person in each pair as either "A" or "B". Have the "B" students cover the sentences and look only at the picture. Have the "A" students ask the "B" students, *"Where is the filing cabinet?"* The "B" students answer. When they have finished answering all the questions, switch roles.

Review.   Page 125

Fill in your own information.

If possible, make a transparency of the page. Have students fill in their own information. Walk around the room to help students as needed.

Follow-up activity.

Make a copy of the page. For review ask the following questions:

What is your last name?

What is your first name?

What is your address? (street address, city, state, and zip code)

What is your home telephone number?

What is your work telephone number?

What is your date of birth?

Have students fill in the information for their partner.

Listen. Find the letters you hear.

Follow the tape or use the tapescript.

Don't touch! The machine is hot!   Page 126

Pre-listening.

Write the word *sign* on the board.

Have students point to a sign in the classroom.

Next ask students how many signs they see in the picture. *5*

Ask them to name the signs. As they name them, write the words on the board.

Do Not Touch   Exit   Men   Women   Quiet

Ask, *"What kind of a workplace is this?"* If students can't answer, say, *"Is this a school or a factory?" "Are they making clothes or toys?"*

Presentation.

Play the tape or discuss the picture and identify the people shown. Ask students to point to each person as they hear that person's name.

Let's be safe!   Page 127

Play the tape or read the tapescript in the back of the book.

Answers:
1. l   2. d   3. f   4. k   5. c   6. b   7. g   8. e   9. h   10. a   11. j   12. i

Assign workbook page 82.

Answers:	
1. Big trouble! Very dangerous.	7. Emergency! Get out!
2. Go out this way every day.	8. Be careful! Be cautious!
3. Women's restroom	9. Men's restroom
4. This way to the telephone.	10. Don't go in there. (No! Stay out!)
5. Shh-h-h!	11. You can't smoke here.
6. No! Stay out! (Don't go in there.)	12. Danger. Don't touch.

Use workbook page 83.

Do the jazz chants *Watch out, Don't Touch!* and *Signs of the Times.*

They're helping Dad at work.   Page 128

Listen and read.

Play the tape or read the tapescript in the back of the book. Then read each caption aloud and have students repeat after you.

Follow-up activity.

Make a copy of the page.

Have students cut out the pictures without the captions.

Have students create a numbered grid on an 8.5 X 11 inch paper.

Show students how to make a grid of 3 rows and 3 columns by folding their paper in threes, first down, and then across. An easy way to do this is to fold the top section down until it matches the height of the lower half. Then crease it. Next, open the paper and fold up the bottom half to the crease and crease again. Repeat the procedure in the other direction.

Tell students to number the boxes 1 through 9.

Divide the students into small groups. If possible, give each group one file folder or cardboard to use as a barrier.

One student should act as the speaker. The student says, for example, *"I am sending a fax. Box 3."* The other students place the correct picture in the correct box.

The student continues until all pictures are placed on the grid in the right spot. The speaker checks each person's paper.

Rotate speakers and start the process again. Continue until all students have had the chance to be the speaker.

For more advanced students:

The speaker places the pictures on the grid. The speaker says the filing cabinet is on number 1, and then makes sentences such as, *"The filing cabinet is above the clothes-pressing machine."* The students in the group must figure out the number and place the clothes-pressing machine in the right space.

Assign workbook page 84.

Answers:								
1. e	2. c	3. i	4. b	5. a	6. d	7. f	8. h	9. g

Ask your partner.   Pages 129 and 130

Review all the vocabulary on both pages. This includes both the names of people and their actions.

Review the questions: *How do you spell that please?* and *Could you please repeat that?*

Review the question: *What is _____ doing?*

Follow the directions for Information Gap activities in the Introduction.

Assign workbook page 85 and 86.

What about you. Where are you? What are you doing now? Answers will vary.

This activity can be used for a student-produced publication. Guide students to write about themselves at school, work, or home. Have students pair off and read their stories to each other. Model this by using your own story. If there is a computer available in the class or if there is a computer lab, have students word process their stories. Pairs may check for beginning and end punctuation. Print the stories out and display them in the classroom. You may prefer to develop a class book for each student of all finished stories. If a camera is available, pictures of students can be taken and placed with individual stories.

Review   Page 131

Ask students to complete this page independently.

I can do this!   Page 132

Follow the general directions in the Introduction.
Assign the Crossword Puzzle and Wordsearch, Workbook pages 87 and 88.

UNIT 11 *Crossword Puzzle*

 UNIT 11 *Wordsearch*

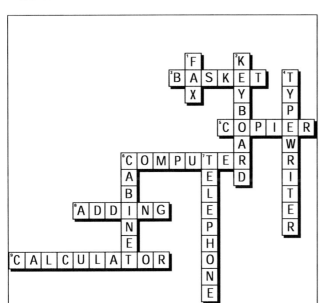

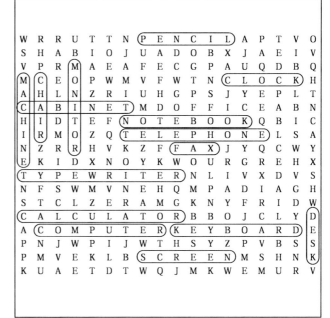

What's the problem? Page 133

Presentation.

For general suggestions about how to use this page refer to the Introduction. Always ask the general questions about the illustration before moving on to the more specific questions suggested for each unit. (See specific questions for this unit below.)

For most beginning students:

Use a transparency, if available. If not, use the text.

Ask, *"Are they in a house or a school?" house*

For low beginning students:

Are there three rooms or two rooms? *3 rooms*

Is there a bathroom or a bedroom in the picture? *bathroom*

Is there water in the kitchen or in the living room? *kitchen*

For beginning students:

Is this a two room apartment? *No, it is three rooms.*

Is there a problem in the bathroom? *Yes, there is.*

Is the kitchen fine? *No, it has a problem, too.*

For more advanced students:

How many rooms are there? *3*

What is wrong in the bathroom? *The toilet isn't working. (It's overflowing.)*

What is wrong in the kitchen? *The refrigerator isn't working. (It's leaking.)*

Listen and read.

Read the paragraph aloud as students follow along. Ask them to follow the direction and fill in the sentence that is incomplete. Point to the static on the TV and say, *"No picture."*

Point to the toilet and say it is overflowing. Write *overflowing* on the board. Point to the refrigerator and say, *"It is leaking."* Write *leaking* on the board. Ask students to talk about problems they have in their homes. Some problems they may have are leaky ceilings, cockroaches, electrical problems, leaky faucets, etc. Develop a list of home problems on the board.

The roof is leaking.   Page 134

Play the tape or read the tapescript in the back of the book.

Have students listen and follow along and then listen again and read each sentence after you. After each sentence ask, *"Why is that a problem?"* Give help to students in expressing their ideas. Reword, if necessary, in correct English and write your sentences on the board.

Follow-up activity.

Copy the page and have students cut out the pictures. Using the nine square grid they drew for the follow-up activity on page 128 of Unit 11, have students practice the same activity. Use the same directions.

The window is cracked.   Page 135

Review the sentences at the top of the page with students.

Using an overhead projector or the text, have students point to each problem as you say it.

Next, divide the students into pairs and have them practice pointing to the picture as a partner says the problem.

Have students write the sentences for each problem in the spaces provided.

Answers:	
1. The roof is leaking.	6. The television isn't working.
2. The window is cracked.	7. The heat isn't working.
3. The faucet is dripping.	8. The shower isn't working.
4. The toilet is overflowing.	9. The refrigerator is leaking.
5. The stove is broken.	

Assign workbook page 89.

Workbook answers:					
1. yes	3. no	5. yes	7. no	9. no	11. no
2. no	4. yes	6. no	8. yes	10. yes	12. no

Yes, I'm the manager.   Page 136

Divide students into pairs and have them practice the conversation. Then ask them to substitute the different problems pictured below the conversation in **Practice.** Encourage them to expand the conversation by adding one or two more problems.

Follow-up activity.

If possible, give each group a tape recorder and a blank cassette tape. Have the groups record each member practicing the dialog. Play the tapes and let the students hear how they sound. While they are recording, walk around and help individuals who have pronunciation problems.

Who fixes the problems?   Page 137

Write the words *plumber, repairperson, electrician,* and *TV repairperson* on the board. Make sure students understand these occupations.

Ask students, *"What do you do when you have a problem in your apartment or house?"*

For students who rent, find out how many call the manager, write the manager, or fix the problem themselves. Find out what language they use with their manager.

If possible, make a transparency of the page. Follow the tape or read the tapescript in the back of the book.

Have students think of a problem that they have or have had (or ask them to make up a problem) and write an imaginary note to the manager.

Divide students into small groups and have them share their notes.

Assign workbook page 90.

> *Answers will vary.*
>
> Tell students to make up an apartment number, such as 201-A and to refer to the art before they fill in the letters to the manager.

The stove is broken.   Page 138

Presentation.

Make an overhead transparency or refer to the text.

With the class make a list of 9 problems shown on the page. (The stove is broken., The heat isn't working., The TV isn't working., The faucet is dripping., The ceiling is leaking., The toilet is overflowing., The refrigerator is leaking., The shower is broken., and The window is cracked.)

Divide students into pairs and have them practice the conversation by substituting the problems shown pictured in 1–9.

Follow-up activity.

Make copies of the page and have students cut out the pictures. Have each student choose one problem. Have students mingle around the room practicing the conversation about their particular problem. The student approached should ask, *"What's the problem?"* If possible, that student should suggest whom to call.

Use workbook page 91.

Do the jazz chant *What's the problem?* by following the directions in the Introduction.

We need to move.   Page 139

Presentation.

Write the word *move* on the board. Ask students, *"When did you move last? How many times have you moved?"* Elicit answers from various students.

Find out why people need to move. Some possible reasons: to be near family, for work, for convenience, for a bigger/smaller place, for more money, etc.

Read and answer the questions.

> *Answers:*
>
> 1. He has too many problems.
> 2. They want to move to a house.
> 3. To look at ads for a house.
> 4. The window is broken, the toilet is overflowing, and the refrigerator is leaking.
>
> **Note:** A broken TV is not usually considered a problem for the manager to fix.

The Spring Valley News.   Page 140

Ask students how they find an apartment for rent.

Possible responses are: through a real estate agent, a friend, a For Rent sign, a newspaper.

Make a transparency of the page or refer to the text.

Tell students that José and Carlos are going to look in the newspaper for a house. Tell them that these ads are called *"Classified Ads."* Have the students repeat the words after you a few times.

Read each ad aloud. Clarify any new words.

Have students answer the 7 questions.

Answers:			
1. 2	3. It is an apartment.	5. Yes	7. $325
2. Yes	4. Yes	6. Yes	

Assign workbook page 92.

Answers:
1. C   2. D   3. E   4. A, G   5. B   6. B   7. F

Talk about it.   Page 141

Use an overhead transparency or use the text. Review each ad.

Ask questions similar to those on Page 140.

Listen to the tape or read the tapescript with students.

Pair students and have them practice answering each of the 7 ads.

Follow-up activity.

Bring the real classified rental housing section from your local newspaper to class. Make enough copies for each student, if possible.

Have each student review the ads and choose one they might be interested in.

Pair students and have them role play and call and ask their partner about the apartment or house.

Assign workbook page 93.

Answers:
A. 1. h   2. g   3. b   4. i   5. f   6. e   7. a   8. c   9. d   B. Answers will vary.

New house for rent.   Page 142

Pre-reading.

Elicit as much information about the picture as possible. Discuss with students who the woman is. (a real estate agent)

Use the tape if available or read aloud and have students read along.

Discuss what an appropriate rent would be for this house by using the classified ads from the previous follow-up activity.

Have students find a similar house and note the rents. Assign a rent to the house pictured.

Do you like this house?   Page 143

Elicit as much information about the picture as possible. Some points to elicit include:

How many bedrooms are there?

What rooms are upstairs? What rooms are downstairs?

Where is the living room? Where is the kitchen? Does it have a big or small yard?

How many cars can fit in the garage?

Use the tape or ask each question and have students answer.

Answers:

1. 1	2. 2	3. Yes	4. bathroom	5. Yes	6. Yes	7. No	8. Yes

Practice. Interview your classmate.

Have students interview each other and write in the number for each item. With the whole class discuss the numbers for each item.

Assign workbook page 94.

Answers:

1. rent	3. one	5. tub	7. stove	9. garage
2. three	4. two	6. shower	8. refrigerator	10. bedrooms

I can do this!   Page 144

Follow the general directions in the Introduction.

Assign the Crossword Puzzle and Wordsearch, Workbook pages 95 and 96.

 UNIT 12 *Crossword Puzzle*

 UNIT 12 *Wordsearch*

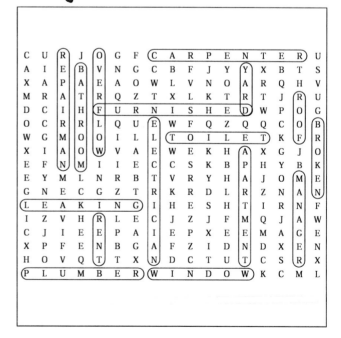

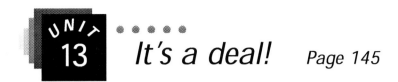

Presentation.

For general suggestions about how to use this page refer to the Introduction. Always ask the general questions about the illustration before moving on to the more specific questions suggested for each unit. (See specific questions for this unit below.)

For most beginning students:

Are they inside or outside the house? *outside*

Are the men happy or sad? *happy*

Is the woman a real estate agent or a teacher? *real estate agent*

For low beginning students:

Are they outside the house? *Yes, they are.*

Are the men sad? *No. They are happy.*

Is the real estate agent shaking hands with one man? *Yes.*

For more advanced students:

Where are they? *They are outside the house.*

How do the men feel? *They are happy.*

Why is the real estate agent shaking hands? *Because the men are renting the house.*

Ask students to close their books. Have students practice the dialog by following the tape or by reading along as you read the dialog aloud.

Have students circle the correct answers.

Answers:

    1. No   2. No   3. b   4. b

    They need to go to the bank to get money to pay the rent; they need to go to the post office to change their address; they need to go to City Hall to turn on their utilities (water, gas, and electric).

Note: Turning on your utilities varies by location. If you do not go to City Hall for your utilities to be turned on, discuss with students where they would go to have their water, gas, and electricity turned on.

Assign workbook page 97.

Answers: Part A

    1. like   2. rent   3. happy   4. excited   5. is 6. "It's a deal!" 7. good

Part B

    José and Carlos like the house they saw. They want to rent the house. They are happy. They are also excited. The price is right. They say, "It's a deal!" It is a good house for them.

Carlos goes to the bank.   Page 146

Have students follow along with the tape or read the tapescript in the back of the book.

Follow-up activity.

Copy the page and have students cut out the pictures. Using the 9-square grid they drew for the follow-up activity on page 128 of Unit 11, have students practice the same activity. Use the same directions.

Need some money?   Page 147

Review the words at the side of the page with students.

Using an overhead transparency or the text, have students point to the words as you say them.

Next have students write the correct words for the money items pictured.

Answers:

1. ATM machine	3. cash	5. money order	7. check
2. credit card	4. checking account	6. ATM card	

Assign workbook page 98.

Workbook answers: Part B

1. check	3. checking account	5. ATM card	7. cash
2. ATM machine	4. credit card	6. cash	

Follow-up activity.

Have students answer the following questions:

Do you use a bank? What do you use the bank for?

Do you have a savings account?

Do you have a checking account?

Do you have an ATM card?

Do you have a credit card?

Do you have a debit card? Explain that some banks have debit cards which look like a credit card but are like an ATM card. (If your local area does not have debit cards, ignore this question.)

Have students make a grid of six rows and five columns. Have them put a students name at the top of each column. They should interview five students asking the 5 or 6 questions above.

I need a money order.   Page 148

Read the copy at the top of the page in which the man expresses a need for a money order. Then read aloud the first sentence and call on a volunteer to read the correct response aloud. Tell students to continue reading and matching the other items.

Answers:

1. e	2. d	3. b	4. a	5. c	6. f	7. g

Follow-up activities.

Write either a sentence or a response on a strip of paper. Hand out the strips and have students find their partner. Collect strips and redistribute until all students in the class have had a chance to practice. Elicit from students where (the location) and when (the occasion) they might ask each question or express a need.

Can I have a Change of Address form?   Page 149

Discuss the picture. Ask students to identify where people are (at the Duttonville Post Office.) Write the words *stamps, letter, package, Change of Address form, postcard* and *money order* on the board. Make sure students understand these words. You may wish to bring in the actual objects to show students.

If possible, make a transparency of the page. Follow the tape or read the tapescript in the back of the book.

Play the tape or read the tapescript again and ask students to underline each word as they hear it.

What do you need at the post office?   Page 150

Review each of the items listed on the page. Have students match each word with the correct picture.

Answers:		
1. d package	3. a letter	5. b postcard
2. e stamps	4. f money order	6. c Change of Address form

Assign workbook page 99.

Answers:			
1. letter	2. stamps	3. package	4. Change of Address form

I need to mail a package.   Page 151

Presentation.

Make an overhead transparency or refer to the text.

With the class make a list of all the reasons they go to the post office: mail a package, buy stamps, mail a letter, to change their address, to buy a money order. (Find out if students use the post office to buy money orders or if they go to a place that cashes checks.) Review each sentence on the left. Find out if any of the students said any of these sentences (or had a need to say them) recently. Then have the students match the response for each sentence on the left.

Answers:					
1. b	2. c	3. e	4. f	5. a	6. d

Where can you buy money orders?   Page 152

Presentation.

Write the words *money order* on the board. Ask students, *"Did you ever buy a money order?"* Find out how much it cost. Be sure that students know that to send one to their country they buy an international money order. Be sure they understand that they need to save the receipts to get their money back if it gets lost and does not arrive at the proper destination.

Have students write today's date on the line provided.

Next, have them write the name of someone in their country.

Pair students and have them tell their partner to make out a money order for them. Students may need to spell their name for *pay to* and decide on the amount of the money order.

Review the pronunciation of each number shown on the page.

Follow-up activity.

Have a money dictation. Select five amounts and dictate them to the class. Next pair students; have each student write five amounts and dictate them to their partners.

Sample amounts: $1,025, $533, $34.02, $679.82, $1,125.43.

Assign workbook page 100.

Ask your partner.   Pages 153 and 154

Review the vocabulary on both pages.

Review the question: *Could you please repeat that?*

Follow the directions for Information Gap activities in the Introduction.

Answers:			
1. check	4. ATM card	7. stamps	10. money order
2. credit card	5. cash	8. letter	11. postcard
3. money order	6. change of address	9. ATM machine	12. package

Assign workbook page 101.

It'll be very cold next month.   Page 155

Ask students where Carlos and José are. Again discuss where students pay their utility bills. Also discuss where they go to get their utilities turned on. Make sure that all students understand how to turn on their utilities.

Follow the tape or read aloud **Listen and read.** Have students follow along silently. Then have them decide which month they think it is (perhaps October or November). Talk about utility costs. Elicit from students about how much they pay for utilities. Find out who pays for water separately and who doesn't. Have students speculate on the month that José's wife and daughter will move to Duttonville.

Do the jazz chant *It's a Deal* on workbook page 101. Follow the directions in the Introduction.

I can do this! Page 156

Follow the general directions in the Introduction.

Assign the Crossword Puzzle and Wordsearch, Workbook pages 103 and 104.

 UNIT 13 *Crossword Puzzle*

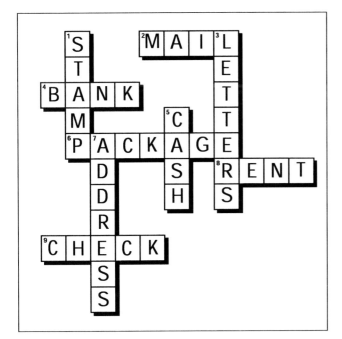

UNIT 13 *Wordsearch*

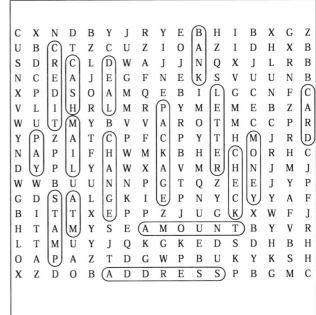

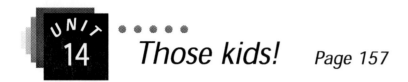

Presentation.

For general suggestions about how to use this page refer to the Introduction. Always ask the general questions about the illustration before moving on to the more specific questions suggested for each unit. (See specific questions for this unit below.)

For most beginning students:

Are they inside or outside the house? *inside*

Is Rose happy or upset? *upset*

Is Bic reading or eating potato chips? *eating potato chips*

Is Kim talking on the phone or reading? *talking on the phone*

For low beginning students:

Are they outside the house? *No.*

Is Rose upset? *Yes.*

Is Bic reading? *No. He's eating potato chips.*

Is Kim talking on the phone? *Yes.*

For more advanced students:

Where are they? *They are at home.*

How does Rose feel? *She is upset.*

What is Bic doing? *He is on the couch eating potato chips.*

What is Kim doing? *She's talking on the phone.*

Write the words *lazy, messy, noisy, makeup* and *short* on the board.

Discuss each word to make sure students know the meaning.

Have students close their books and have them practice the dialog by following the tape or the tapescript.

Ask the question, *"What do you think about Rose and her son and daughter?"* Have a short discussion about the situation. by asking the following questions:

- Do you think Kim's skirt is too short?
- Should Bic be eating potato chips and lying on the couch?
- Should teenage girls wear makeup?
- Can Rose change her children's behavior? How?

Assign workbook page 105.

Answers:

Part A

    1. Rose 2. lazy 3. doesn't look   4. is   5. doesn't come 6. drives   7. smokes

Part B

Rose is upset with Bic. Bic is lazy at home. He doesn't look clean. Bic's room is messy. Bic comes home late. He drives too fast. He smokes too much.

Are you angry? Are you pleased?   Page 158

Make an overhead transparency or use the text.

Have students follow along with the tape or use the tapescript.

Review the words orally again with the class. Make sure that students understand the meanings of all the words. If students do not readily see that a. and b. are opposites, dramatize an angry person and a pleased person for the class. Invite volunteers to select other pairs of words that are opposites and perform actions to demonstrate their opposite meanings.

Have students complete the sentences at the bottom of the page with any words that are appropriate.

Follow-up activity.

Copy the page and have students cut out the pictures. Using the 9-square grid they drew for the follow-up activity on page 128, Unit 11, have students practice the same activity. Use the same directions.

Alternate follow-up activity.

Cut out the pictures and glue each one on an index card. Have a total physical response activity.

Give each student a pair of scissors, a glue stick, and 16 index cards. Tell students to cut out each picture, but not the words, and glue each picture on an index card.

Put students into small groups. Use only one set of cards. Play "Go Fish" or "Concentration" with the cards. Tell students that two cards with opposite meanings make a pair.

    Go Fish

    Deal out the cards.

    Each player in turn asks the other players for a card depicting an adjective.

    If a player has the card asked for he/she gives it to the person who asked. If not, the player can say "Go fish."

    Players try to make pairs of cards.

    Concentration

    Spread all the cards face down on a table.

    Turn cards over two at a time.

    Collect all pairs.

    The player with the most pairs wins.

Assign workbook page 105.

Bic drives too fast.   Page 159

Review the adjectives on the page. Have students circle the answers that they think to be true about each character named. Have them check answers with their partner.

Next have them think about the words that apply to them. Have them share with a partner.

Answers:			
1. fast	3. dirty	5. hard-working	7. late
2. upset	4. too much	6. messy	8. noisy

Practice.

Ask students to complete the **Practice** section on their own.

Assign workbook page 106. Then invite volunteers to read aloud for the class what they wrote for **B. Write about you.**

Who likes what?   Page 160

Review the word groups. Ask students to name one thing that Rose doesn't like. Then elicit the opposite response by asking, *"Well, what does Rose like?"* Students should assume the opposite response based on what they know about each character.

Assign workbook page 107.

A. Explain to students that they should mingle and ask classmates these questions: *"Do you like fast cars?" "Are you quiet?" "Do you like to talk on the phone?" "Do you like a lot of make-up?"* If a classmate responds *Yes,* to the first question for example, the interviewer should write the name of the classmate in the first space under **Name.** Point out that the person's name and the words on the right, *likes fast cars,* will form a complete sentence. If the classmate responds *No* to the first question, the interviewer should write the name of the classmate in the second space under **Name** to complete the sentence, _____ *doesn't like fast cars.* Tell the students to then go on to the next question, *"Are you quiet?"* and repeat the procedure.

B. Model the first two sentences. Make sure students understand that the *I* in each sentence is you (or someone else) telling about likes and dislikes. Answers will vary.

Practice.

Review the words with students.

Next have partners discuss what Bic and Rose like and don't like.

Answers will vary. Encourage students to add a few extra likes and dislikes based on what they know about the individual characters.

Follow-up activity.

Have students make charts on classmates' likes and dislikes similar to those they did for Bic, Rose, and Kim.

Take a message.   Page 161

Make an overhead transparency or use the text.

Ask students if they ever take messages in English over the phone.

Use the focused listening technique and have students repeat the correct phone number.

Have students follow along with the tape or use the tapescript.

Have students write the message. Tell students to make up a time, such as 5 P.M.

Answers:
    For: Kim
    From: Stacy
    Time: (Answers will vary.)
    Please call.
    Phone: (702)555-9702

Hello, can I speak to . . . ?   Page 162

First have several student pairs practice the top telephone dialog for the class. Then pair students and have them practice making phone calls and taking messages. The students who are taking the messages should have their books closed. If possible, give students message slips so they can write the messages.

Follow-up activity.

If it's feasible, have students call your office or home and leave a message on your answering machine.

Assign workbook page 108.

Do the jazz chants *This or That?* and *Taking the Message* following the directions in the Introduction.

Ask your partner.   Pages 163 and 164

If possible bring in an answering machine and discuss its use and usefulness. Review the messages on pages 163 and 164.

Review all the vocabulary on both pages.

Follow the directions for Information Gap activities in the Introduction.

Answers: Pages 163 and 164
    1. For: Margo, From: Louisa, 2:30, April 5, (405) 555-1191, Please call me.
    2. For: Mother, From: Ibrahim, 4:00 PM, Tuesday, (no phone number)
    3. For: Kay, From: Grace, 4:30, Wednesday, (714) 555-5111, Please call when you get in.
    4. For: Van Ly, From: Ms. Apple, 6:30 PM, Monday evening, 555-8360, If you can't come to school, please call me.

You kids!   Page 165

Listen and read.

Look at the picture and say, *"What does Rose not like about her kids?"*

Elicit from students things that Rose doesn't like.

Follow the tape or use the tapescript.

Review any words that might be new by writing them on the board and helping students to understand them.

Listen and write the word.

Follow the tape or use the tapescript or read the text as students follow along.

Answers:			
1. short	3. thin	5. fast	7. curly
2. long	4. heavy	6. slow	8. straight

Follow-up activity.

Add new adjectives to the previously-created index card set. Again, students can play "Go Fish" or "Concentration" at this time.

Kim likes makeup!   Page 166

Review parts of the body. Be sure to discuss all the words that are listed on page 166.

Use the focused-listening technique described in the Introduction.

Before opening the book, give students crayons or colored markers and a copy of Kim and have them add the makeup as they listen to the paragraph.

Follow the tape or use the tapescript. Have students write the correct word under each picture.

Answers:				
1. neck	3. eyes	5. mouth	7. teeth	9. cheek
2. ear	4. eyebrow	6. eyelashes	8. nose	

Review.   Page 167

Make an overhead transparency of the page or use a student text.

Review all the body parts.

Have students write in the correct words.

Assign workbook pages 109 and 110. Answers will vary.

Have students carry out the drawing and labeling instructions in **A-B.** Then ask them to complete the sentences in **C.** Give help as needed. Before students begin **D.**, discuss what something special about yourself" means. Explain to students that each person is "special" and unique because of talents and abilities to do things or act in a certain way. They may wish to mention some physical characteristic, an ability to perform well in a sport, a talent to paint, dance well, etc., or perhaps a personality trait that others appreciate in them. Encourage students to think of any one special thing about themselves that makes them happy and proud. If students are reluctant to write something, encourage them by asking leading questions.

I can do this! Page 168

Follow the general directions given in the Introduction.

Assign the Crossword Puzzle and Wordsearch, Workbook pages 111 and 112.

 UNIT 14 *Crossword Puzzle*

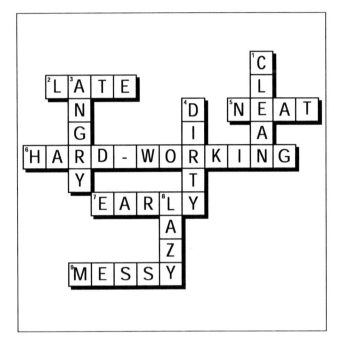

 UNIT 14 *Wordsearch*

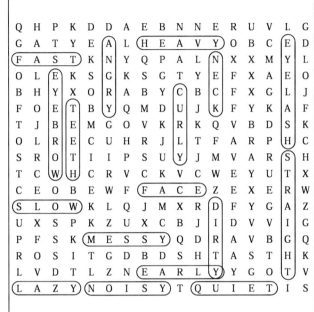

José and Carlos are having a party.

Page 169

Presentation.

For general suggestions about how to use this page refer to the Introduction. Always ask the general questions about the illustration before moving on to the more specific questions suggested for each unit. (See specific questions for this unit below.)

Point to the two boys in the picture who are standing and say, "This is Carlos and José."

For most beginning students:

Are they in a house or a classroom? *(classroom)*

Are Carlos and José sitting or standing? *(standing)*

Are the students studying or listening? *(listening)*

For low beginning students:

Are they in a classroom? *(Yes, they are.)*

Are Carlos and José sitting? *(No, they aren't. They're standing and talking to the class.)*

Are the students studying? *(No they aren't. They're listening to Carlos and José.)*

For more advanced students:

Where are they? *They're in the classroom.*

What are Carlos and José doing? *They're standing and talking to the class.*

What are the students doing? *They're listening to Carlos and José.*

Discuss what Carlos and José might be talking about.

Write the word *party* on the board.

Brainstorm with students about occasions when they have parties.

> Find out if they have parties when they move into a new house.
>
> Ask them what do they do when they move into a new house.
>
> Write the word *housewarming* on the board.
>
>> Tell students in the United States, it is typical for people to have a housewarming when they move into a new house.
>>
>> Guests bring something to add to the new house—perhaps a plant, a picture, or a vase.
>
> Next write the word *potluck* on the board.
>
>> Elicit the meaning of *potluck* from the students. If no one knows the answer, discuss it with them.
>>
>> Explain that a potluck dinner or party is an American tradition. Everyone brings one dish to share with others who are present.

Follow the tape or read aloud each of the four items along with choices a. and b.

Answers:			
1. a	2. a	3. a	4. b

A celebration!   Page 170

Presentation.

Make a transparency of the page or use the text.

Using a piece of paper to cover the page, reveal one picture at a time and ask, *"What are they celebrating?"*

Continue until you have finished with all four pictures.

Follow the tape or read the captions under the pictures.

Follow-up activity.

Help students to make a table on paper or in their notebook. The table should have 4 columns and 5 rows.

Name	End of School Party	Housewarming	Potluck

Tell students to ask four other people the following questions. Write each person's name and either *Yes* or *No* in each frame. Tell students to insert their own information in the last row.

Do you have end-of-school parties in your country?

Did you have a housewarming when you moved into your house?

Do you like or think you would like a potluck party?

Have students complete a class chart including everyone's information.

Assign workbook page 113.

Answers:

1. potluck   2. housewarming   3. end of the school term   4. celebration

When do you have it?   Page 171

Make an overhead transparency or use the text.

Point to each picture. Say, *"What kind of party is it?"* Have students complete each sentence.

Elicit from the class some other types of celebrations there are in their country.

Write the celebrations on the board and have students copy them on the lines provided in the text.

Answers:

a. housewarming   b. end of school term   c. potluck   d. celebration

Answers will vary for the **Practice** activity.

Assign workbook page 114. Answers will vary.

What year is it?   Page 172

Make a transparency or use the text.

Have students fill in the calendar according to the current year.

Next brainstorm with them to come up with various holidays and write the dates on the board. Have students circle them on the calendar.

Follow-up activity.

Compare holidays.

Have students talk about holidays in their country. Then make a list of the holidays and the dates on which they celebrate these holidays. Make sure you talk about the many different dates of New Year's around the world.

What other celebrations?   Page 173

Review the ways we express dates orally (as ordinal numbers) by saying each date on the January calendar (January first, January second, and so on.)

Also review the expressions, the first Monday, the last Thursday, the third Monday, etc.

Presentation.

Make a transparency of the page or use the text.

Point to each picture and say the name of the holiday. Have the students read after you.

Find out which holidays they are familiar with and help them understand the ones that are new to them.

Discuss the fact that some holidays use the lunar calendar and don't come at the same time every year. The holidays that use the lunar calendar include: Hanukkah, Ramadan, Chinese Tet New Year, and Easter.

Have students write the correct date under each picture.

Then ask them to circle the dates on the calendar on page 172.

Answers:	
1. January 1	9. Last Monday in May
2. The third Monday in January	10. July 4
3. varies	11. November 11
4. varies	12. October 31
5. The third Monday in February	13. Third Monday in October
6. February 14	14. The last Thursday in November
7. varies	15. First Monday in September
8. varies	16. December 25

Follow-up activity.

Copy the page and have students cut out the pictures. Using the 9-square grid they drew for the follow-up activity on page 128, Unit 11, have students practice the same activity, using the the same directions.

José and his family go shopping for party food.   Page 174

Presentation.

Make a transparency or use the text.

Discuss the pictures with the students and elicit as much vocabulary about it as possible.

Follow the tape or read the tapescript in the back of the book.

Brainstorm with the class ideas for food José and his family might buy for the party.

Divide students into groups and have them decide on one dish that a guest could bring.

Have each group generate a shopping list for the ingredients for that dish.

It's your choice.   Page 175

Follow the tape or use the tapescript in the back of the book.

Listen and underline the words you hear:			
meat and rice	pita bread	egg rolls	tortillas
hot dogs	sandwiches	salad	sushi
chips	pizza	juice	

Have students list on the lines provided some of the foods they take to parties.

Follow-up activity.

If feasible, start planning a potluck party for the end of the semester. Make a class list of foods, decide on the date, etc.

Assign workbook pages 115, 116, and 117.

Answers: Page 115B	
1. pancakes, salsa, hot dogs	3. egg rolls, rice, hot dogs
2. pita bread, pizza, salsa	4. rice, salad, sushi
Answers: Page 116B (continued)	
5. sushi, egg rolls, pancakes	6. hot dogs, salad, potato chips
Answers: Page 117	
Answers will vary.	

Let's get ready!   Page 176

Make an overhead transparency of the page or use the text.

Ask students, *"Who do you see in the picture?"*   *"Grandpa."*

Read the words near the picture and ask students to repeat them. Make sure that students understand them.

Listen and write.

Play the tape or read the tapescript. Pause wherever a word is missing to allow students time to fill in the blanks. Then invite volunteers to read aloud the story about Grandpa.

Are you ready yet?   Page 177

Presentation.

Review the vocabulary on the page.

Review the question: *Could you please repeat that?*

Divide students into pairs. Direct each student in a pair to look at either the pictures only or the words only. Have students fold the page lengthwise or else have them cover one column with a sheet of paper.

Partner *answers:*

    1.e   2. a   3. b   4. c   5. d

Word under the picture *answers:*

    1. shaving   3. brushing teeth   5. getting dressed

    2. taking a shower   4. combing hair

Follow-up activity.

Have students make a list of the order in which they do the above activities in the morning.

School is out!   Page 178

Listen and read.

Point to the picture and ask, *"What kind of party do you think this is?"*

Encourage students to discuss the illustration by naming various things they see and the action that is taking place.

Follow the tape or read the text.

Review any words in the text that students might not know.

Assign workbook page 118.

Follow-up activity.

Have a class party!

Certificate of Completion   Page 179

Review the vocabulary with the students. Either choose to fill out the complete certificate for each student or have them fill out the information about themselves. Then sign the certificate for each student.

I can do this!   Page 180

Follow the general directions in the Introduction.

Assign the Crossword Puzzle and Wordsearch, Workbook pages 119 and 120.

UNIT 15 Crossword Puzzle

UNIT 15 Wordsearch

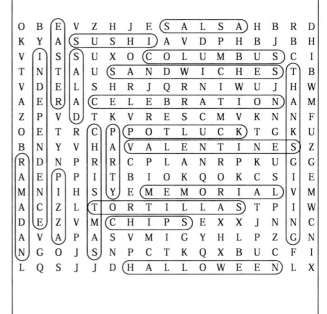